T0353139

Flood Cycle: Notes from a Changing Planet

Also by John Kelly –
Due South: An Antarctic Journal

FLOOD CYCLE

Notes from a Changing Planet

by

John Kelly

Signal Books
Oxford

First published in 2009 by
Signal Books Limited
36 Minster Road
Oxford
OX4 1LY
www.signalbooks.co.uk

A catalogue record for this book is available from the British Library.

ISBN 978-1-904955-59-7 Paper

Production: Devdan Sen
Cover Design: Devdan Sen
Cover Images: John Kelly
Photographs: all photographs © John Kelly, except: p.41, courtesy National
Gallery, London; p.87 courtesy Anchorage Museum Archives; p.93 courtesy
Joseph C. von Fischer; p.101 courtesy Tizzy Consortium Library, Barrow;
p.118 courtesy Roderick Thorne

Printed in India

CONTENTS

Preface
page vi

Acknowledgements
page viii

I
The Tropospheric World
Bolivia and Newfoundland
page 1

II
The Hercynian Forest
Finland and the Baltic Sea
page 31

III
Ice Bears and Time Lines
Svalbard, Norway
page 47

IV
Whale Spirits and Trampolines
Alaska
page 73

V
The Orcadian Sea
The Orkney Islands
page 103

Preface

During the three years it has taken to compile these notes I have increasingly come to realise that change is part of the natural order. We live on a complex planet, where observations may be happenchance and unexpected, reflecting the sometimes ponderous path of geological and climatic change. To see something clearly we need to be able to detach from it and place ourselves at a distance. Some years ago earth was seen rising from the lunar surface: it was a dramatic moment in our understanding of the planet. These 'notes' were, on a number of occasions, written within isolated and remote locations. They chronicle six individual journeys taken in parts of the world where climate change is already having an effect upon people's lives.

Some time ago I wrote a brief description of a storm as it unleashed its force upon the coast of Sussex. I had sheltered by the fallen chalk of the Telscombe cliffs, as rain and wind had battered the vertical wall of rock. Recently, I returned to the same beach. A high tide covered the boulders where I had placed myself on the earlier visit. The line of cliffs had altered and the coloration of the chalk had changed. A dark green covering of moss traced a section where, as I recall, a waterfall had cascaded to the shore, fed by the torrential rain. A sequence of rock fall and collapse had produced piles of broken chalk, extending out into a choppy sea, causing the water to assume a white density. The years had clearly seen the transformation of this particular stretch of coast.

In 'Flood Cycle' the recording of moments in time has produced a number of observations or epiphanies, and like unfolding scenes, they should be read as individual events. The choice of location for the journeys has been guided in large part by a number of art residency programmes. These have arrowed towards the north, as if pursuing some furthest point. However, this northern path has been set by the dramatic changes that are occurring on our planet, particularly with melting sea ice, and it is here that a number of science groups are intent on gaining an understanding of these changes.

In the course of three years I have flown above the great expanses of the northern snows, piecing together a mental map of ice surfaces. A collective impression of the dwindling ice sheets and mountain glaciers stays with me. I retain a hold of these high latitudes as they slant polewards into the perpetual light of northern summers. From these elevated views the story of ice can be read as a busy traffic of glacial migration, with its relentless processes of advance and retreat. The peeling away of the skin of ice that we witness today has exposed vast areas of tundra to the fresh light of day. Standing upon these new surfaces I have, more than once, looked north to see a sharp white line of ice as it continues its poleward journey. Standing at Point Barrow I was able to look across the Beaufort Sea towards the islands of Svalbard; a straight line passing over the top of the world and through the pole to a familiar shore where I had stood twelve months previously. That year had seen a further melting away of sea ice producing an almost ice free sea during the summer months. The residency programmes have given me access to some of the finest science organisations. They have shown that we do indeed live on a complex planet, full of interacting systems. From their work we are presented with a picture of rapid transformation, both climatic and environmental. The work of science has established a way forward, and we ignore this at our peril.

While these 'notes' are an endorsement of the picture presented by scientific research, they are primarily the result of those chance encounters made in remote places. Sometimes we need to listen to the song of the earth, to observe those traces of change and to place ourselves within the domain of wild creatures.

John Kelly
Brighton 2008

Acknowledgements

My thanks go to Arts Council England for providing the financial support for the Flood Cycle project and also to the Tyndall Centre for Climate Change for their guidance on the problems facing the coastal regions of Britain and, on a wider scale, the global implications for the future. Further support has come from the Natural Environmental Research Council (NERC), British Antarctic Survey (BAS) and the Scott Polar Research Institute (SPRI). In particular, I would like to thank Nick Cox of BAS for the sharing of his considerable experience of the Arctic and also Heather Lane of SPRI who, from the start of the project, has offered both encouragement and support. I would also like to acknowledge the various residency programmes and those associated with them, including Asher Minns of the Tyndall Centre for Climate Change, Anne Marceau of the Gros Morne National Park in partnership with the Newfoundland and Labrador Art Gallery, Katarina Gaddnas of the Aland artists programme of Finland, Glenn Sheehan of the Barrow Arctic Science Consortium and Dave Nicholls of the Anchorage Museum of History and Art. Thanks also go to the archive departments of SPRI, the Inupiat Heritage Center of Barrow, Kirkwall Library and the Anchorage Museum. The visual work that has resulted from these programmes will form the basis of a number of exhibitions. These venues provided the initial impetus for the whole project and ensured that the various aspects of the work would reach a wide audience. I thank Sophia Wilson of the Cheltenham Museum and Art Gallery, Jeff Horsley of the Manchester Museum and Huw Lewis-Jones of the Scott Polar Research Institute.

A number of friends and associates have been involved during the gathering of the material for this publication and for the ensuing exhibitions. The part they played provided the enjoyment and pleasure to the whole experience. They include Hugh McCormack, Barb Daniell, Bob Martin, Linda Bakken, Dr Roger Worland, Gordana and Yelena, Hugh Broughton, Philip Wells, Sarah Besly, Robert Rhew, Dorcas Stein, Prof. Joseph C. von Fischer, Anita Pensar, Lawrence Rockhill, Satu Kiljunen, Robert Culshaw, Darian La Tocha, Winona Squirrel, Dr Aki Takahashi, Prof. David Walton, Dr John Shears, Tom Muir, John Coll, Dr David Woolf, Prof. Jon Side, Prof. Liz Morris, Priyanka Sharma, Steve Hall, Simon Jude, Roderick Thorne, Dr Sarah Crowe, Santona Goswami, Nelson Parsons, Maria McWilliams, Brian, Laura, Marina, Oscar, Perry and a mongrel by the name of John Franklin.

The Ice

East German Hut. Ny-Alesund, Svalbard

Storms
that roll beneath new skies,
bringing the debris of the past
back from the seabed.

And seas,
active within the initial
light of day.

Here
beneath these skies
a planet turns,
as a hailstorm drags its tendrils of rain
against the cliff face.

Telscombe Beach. Sussex. 2000.

If a natural theology exists, then the atmospheric power of storms and
lightning must stand at the apex of that belief.

Leonardo da Vinci.

Part One
The Tropospheric World

Bolivia and Newfoundland

Sketch the First.

On the internal structure of cloud mass.

Rising and fragmenting, held not in graceful suspension but in convecting turmoil.

Each cloud set upon its own planetary path. Each within the perfect symmetry of its atmospheric laws.

Bolivia

Days in Oruro.

Bolivia 2005.
Elevation 12,000'.
Latitude 20 degrees south.

Through the thin gauze I can see the path of cumulus clouds passing overhead. Beneath me hot springs rise into the pool in which I float. The Aguas Terminales lie to the north east of the mining town of Oruro, 12,000' above sea level. A small group of buildings surround the open baths on this exposed surface of the altiplano. The land is flat, with the exception of a small hill that rises beyond the dirt track of a road that ends here at the aguas. Distant columns of dust define the perimeter of the altiplano, as they rise and disperse in the cool air of the afternoon. My suspended state within the cycle of water is assisted by the warm spring as it pumps soft currents of water into the chamber. Occasional conversation from a group of women breaks the calm air as they slowly submerge themselves, fully clothed, into the shallow end of the pool. Buoyancy allows me to float at ease and I continue to look up into the dome of sky. Through the torn fragments of gauze I can see the gradual rise of cloud; towering heads carried in an energetic system.

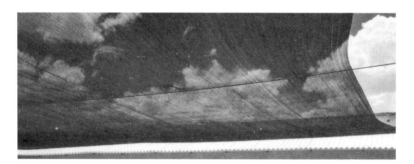

Earlier in the day I had departed from the noise and bustle of La Paz. The bus had risen within the basin, along the steep streets of the capital and through the poverty of El Alto that sprawls out from the city and onto the open land beyond. Most of the people of Bolivia dwell above 10,000' and many of these exist on the harsh, exposed surface of the plain. A steady infill from rivers and glaciers has resulted in the vast elevated world of the Bolivian altiplano. It is a land of thin air and since my arrival I have been gradually allowing my body to become accustomed to the high altitude. However, I have become increasingly aware that at best there are limitations in the exertion levels that one can achieve. Within the streets of La Paz the years of thin air have produced a slow-moving populace and a deceptive calm. Bolivia breathes slowly, unable to sustain a prolonged assault upon its crippling poverty. This poorest of South American countries will, in the next few days, decide upon its destiny through the election of a new president.

The first-ever indigenous candidate, Evo Morales, is set to take power and the streets of the capital are in a state of high excitement. During the night thunder had rolled above the mountain basin. Large raindrops had sounded on the ample skylight above the enclosed courtyard of the hotel and the sound of gunfire could be heard above the rooftops. This morning the flow of traffic, including the colourful microbuses, had been halted by demonstrations of land workers. Above the city clouds had sailed within the basin. Entire systems held constricted by the slopes. The twin dramas of social upheaval and the dynamic path of convecting skies were held together.

The road south led to Oruro as rain produced curtains of water that reduced the outlines of the hills to a blur of vague contours. The small channels intercepted the flow of water, carrying it to the dry stony river beds. The land surface became discoloured by the rain, transforming it to a dark brown terrain beneath the low, brooding sky.

Winds now fluctuate over the heated surface. It is late afternoon. As I remain in the warmth of the spring water, the gauze flutters silently. Dust is carried across the aguas in the thin air and the water surface becomes agitated. The shrill laughter of the women fills the air above the pool. They have come from the old mining town of Oruro and, like some of the children that they have brought with them, are now absorbed in carefree play within the soft water. As I lift myself out of the warmth of the bath so the sharp cool air strikes one side of my body and I clamber over to the shelter of the small changing cubicle. I am reluctant to leave the pleasant sensation of floating in soft warm water. I walk out from the vicinity of the baths onto the surface of the altiplano and make my way up the small hill across the dust track. The land is friable and fractured, scattered with bone and litter. As I stand upon a slight rise I take consecutive photographs of the sky. The eye is drawn to the sky and the insular clouds. The sensation of being within the sky itself is powerful, like a shared existence with these vaporous bodies. I try to estimate cloud height as I look into the cloud structure. By taking further consecutive shots of the cloud in motion I record the great momentum of this upward surging mass. The wind is now carrying the clouds rapidly overhead and I return my gaze to the gravel surface as I reach the crest of the small hill. My wandering is disturbed as I notice two dogs making their way towards me from the empty expanse to the north. I return to the cluster of buildings that form the settlement of Obrajes and join a small group of people awaiting the bus that will take us to Oruro.

Looking from the open window of the bus, I imagine the force lines that generate the hydrological cycle in this elevated world. I am within this mechanism and the slow breath of this cycle can be seen within the minutiae of events as the bus nears Oruro. The mid distance of late afternoon is interrupted by a number of dust columns rising high into the troposphere, carried with the same force that drives the clouds ever higher. Some are violent, with flying debris in their wake, and as we near Oruro so one scatters a group of wild dogs into a frenzied panic, only to leave them chasing the flying plastic bags among the lines of discarded rolling stock. The approach to Oruro is untidy. The debris of tin mining sprawls out beyond the poverty of the outer residential areas. It is a town with a slow echo of past wealth.

20.00 hours. From the roof terrace of Hotel Gran Sucre I observe the fading light of day, once again within the immediate drama of the weather systems. To the east a dense mass of cloud moves slowly along the crest-line of the distant peaks. Beyond these peaks the immensity of the rainforest extends almost two thousand miles to the coast of the Atlantic Ocean. This cloud system has risen from that forest. Within its slow northward journey the towering heads stand vividly against the blue grey of night that is beyond them. Pulses of lightning flicker within the lower levels of this self-energising system, too potent for the solid geometry of the land surface. I draw within the fading light, working quickly to catch the rapid motion of the sky. By drawing the cloud silhouettes in successive sweeps I can measure their speed of change, as they mutate before me. Eventually, nightfall and the dwindling of the sky into the occasional flicker of a passing storm.

Oruro. 18.12.2005. 8.00 hours.

Hotel Gran Sucre is resonant with the glory of the past. Elegant wood-panelled corridors lead to a glass-roofed ballroom that now serves as a breakfast room. Sitting within the splendour of this large room I notice the wall paintings, one of which shows Oruro from some distance across the vast, flat surface of the altiplano. The city hugs the base of ochre toned mountains, seeming to crouch from the constant winds. My perception of the altiplano is still uncertain; this elevated world with its own peculiar atmospheric laws and rarefied air is like a separate time zone, remote and almost forgotten. Beyond the painted landscape canvasses show brass bands, military groups and the familiar unsettling depiction of a nation that has fought tirelessly against the forces of suppression. Today they will vote and I am forced by the blockade on public transport to stay here in Oruro.

Thunder rumbles in the distance, rolling away to the south and the edge of the plain. A day unfolds, fed by the electricity in the air and the momentum of change. Wandering the streets of Oruro I come to the landmark that is the Faro de Conchupata. This folly, in the form of a lighthouse, has no functional value and was constructed in 1851 to commemorate the first raising of the Bolivian flag. This strange political statement is all the more ironic due to the complete lack of coastline within Bolivia, so that this wishful object rises into the thin air like an unattainable dream.

By late afternoon the excitement of the vote has passed. It is that time when a

country holds its breath and waits. The thunderous skies of early morning have gone and the streets of Oruro are now sharply defined in sun and shade, as I return to the roof terrace of the hotel. I am soon engrossed in my sketching and continue the sky studies of the previous evening. Even in an apparent lull the low street of cloud that I study twists and rolls and my page becomes a mass of inter-locking lines. Soon my progress is halted as a curtain of rain and dust passes overhead, sounding aloud on the metal roofs.

As the evening approaches so the din of apparent celebration rises into the air. The illuminated mountain slope beyond the terrace pulses with the electric lights of Christmas from some of the more affluent homes, coming like a power surge from the central core of rock. The mountains' electronic heartbeat continues as the occasional fire cracker cuts the cool evening air. Winds have now abated and the sounds of barking dogs carry across the city. During the night gunshots rose from the slopes of the shanty town. Sounds dispatched across the dark plain to the remote towns and the isolated homesteads, diminished only by the emptiness of distance. In this high realm the people had decided upon their first indigenous leader.

Oruro. 20.12.2005. 9.30 hours.
The Museo Antropológico Eduardo López. The early Twanaku society, while establishing close links with their landscape through the existence of deities, had also spawned the unique practise of skull deformation. The relics of this practice are shown within the main gallery. Glass cases contain the skeletons of the young huddled in death and partially decomposed. The cases are simply constructed and finger smudges blur the clarity of the figures that are contained within them. Drawings on the walls show how the child is held down on a table surface and wedged into an angled clamp. Regular sessions within this device would gradually result in the transition from tabula erecta to the anular oblicua, and therefore placement into the hierarchy of Twanaku society. The ritual is described as the process of trepanation. I move into a small adjacent room and sit by an old photograph that shows ancient terraces still visible and impressed upon a stony slope. The photograph is damaged by water stains but a tracery of past agriculture ghosts through into a sunlit day. From the Spanish text on the information card I discern that here is evidence of an earlier climatic change that is still being played out on the altiplano.

The recurrent phenomena of El Niño, while inflicting flood on the coast of Peru, brings drought to this high country. The forces of the Bolivian water cycle are being diminished and the great surface waters of Lake Titicaca to the north are drying up. The immense salt flats to the south are further evidence of this change. El Niño may be only one of many factors, but when active, stirs at this time of year, and as I sit so I consider the warm waters of the West Pacific drifting east towards the coast of Peru. The affinity between climate change and the fall of civilisations has been witnessed by the Moche people of Northern Peru and, no doubt, by the

8

Inca long before the arrival of the Spanish and the toppling of the weakened mountain state. That flood and drought can co-exist within this Andean world serves to establish a clearer identity for the altiplano, as the effects of the diminishing water cycle can be seen across the open terrain of the plain.

Emerging from the dark interior of the museum I decide to take a taxi to the Lago Uru Uru. This dried lake bed and that of Lago Poopo stretch for over one hundred kilometres to the south of Oruro and eventually fade into the immense surfaces of salt that form the Salar de Coipasa and the Salar de Uyuni. Approaching the lake surface the taxi driver takes a straight road that was at one time the shore of an ancient lake. The surface of the dried lake bed stretches to the south where mirages of floating islands hover tremulously above the cracked surface. I ask the driver to drop me at a discarded wooden shed, requesting that he return in three hours to pick me up. The bewildered driver leaves me within the full glare of the midday sun on a surface of shimmering heat. Flamingo and egret stand in shallow pools of saline water, while overhead, the sky is scattered with cumulus cloud in a vast infinity of blue. I am staggered by the sense of aerial volume and sheer space. Walking out onto the lake bed, impressions within the mud and silt include the delicate footprints of llama and sheep and the thin trace of bird prints, all made when the waters first receded and held them in the hard dry surface. I take a circular walk across the brittle ground, keeping the small wooden hut in sight. At the furthest point of this arc the hut is a mere speck, shimmering within the waves of heat. Eventually I return to the hut with a bag full of bone fragments and various discarded objects that display their tortuous existence within this arid and dying environment.

There is something disorientating about my watch face as I observe the second hand flicker to the designated moment of rendezvous. At the precise time the taxi approaches in a stir of dust and the driver greets me with a smile and a shrug.

Oruro. 20.00 hours.
A storm envelops Oruro. The light of the afternoon has been steadily removed by the arrival of clouds from the eastern cordillera and I make my way along dark streets. The base of the storm touches the rooftops in a cascade of water. To the fluvial accompaniment of the rain I enter the Club Social Croata. The atmosphere is heavy. The club is a grandiose and rambling memento to the days when the world's greatest tin mining area was in its heyday and Oruro must have hummed with affluence. In this evocative interior with its fine panelled and dark walls I sit in total seclusion amid a sea of empty tables. As I eat a light meal of omelette and potatoes I am occasionally disturbed, as suited men pass through the lounge to disappear in the direction of the sound of female laughter.

Oruro. 21.12.2005. 10.00 hours.
The election over and with the restoration of services between Oruro and the south, I board a bus to Cochabamba and commence a journey that will take me to the periphery of the altiplano, including Lake Titicaca in the north and the glaciers of Huayna Potosí in the east. Within these locations the altiplano holds the energy of the water cycle. Bounded by the cordillera of the Andes to the west and east, it is a geography defined by various key points of which Cochabamba, held within the deep valley of the Yungas, offers a glimpse of the immense rainforest that sprawls beyond the eastern mountains of the Cordillera Real and the sacred mountain of Illampu. Occasionally the turbulence of the Amazon rain system rises high upon the slopes of the eastern mountains; a cauldron of spilling air sending the force of warm rain into the lofty rim of the basin.

To the north, the altiplano eventually gives way to the waters of Lake Titicaca, held within a slow process of reduction, as the inland sea responds to changing climate. Storms roll across this high surface, constricted within the mountain domain and forcing ruinous floods upon the shores.

Bolivia

The Altiplano. Moments in Time.

Moments in Time.
Journey Notes. Oruro to Cochabamba.

The transition between climate zones can be sudden, like passing from one room to another, from shade to sunlight. Aware only of an invisible wall of pressure, it is a silent transition, translated through the language of touch and the weight of air.

The long road out from Oruro, beyond the remnants of the Bolivian railway system. We pass an open truck with players from a brass band blowing upon their instruments, sending a shrill cacophony across the fields. Children run towards the bus, waving and laughing. Beyond these scenes the immense plain and the silver thread of pipes carrying water to distant communities. I consider the delusion of maps, that a journey looking so slight on paper can become so vast on the land. Three children sit upon a slight rise, not far from the dust of the road. No word passes between them as they stare ahead into a form of oblivion.

Moments in Time.
Rainforest Notes. Cochabamba.

23.12.2005. Beyond the watershed of the Oriental we enter the broad fertile terrain of Cochabamba. Warmth engulfs the bus, and beyond the dusty windows a scene of tropical colour heralds our arrival into the energy of rain systems. During the night a silent storm of flashing light fills the southern sky, flickering and snaking within the cloud mass, rising from the cover of trees.

24.12.2005. The first rains of the day hit the fine mesh of the canopy, sending down an invisible and cooling spray. With evening a delicate tracery of cloud clings to the mountain slope like frosted wool. Rains drum on the tin roofs during the night, cascading into the central courtyard.

25.12.2005. With morning, grey low cloud hangs over the town. Buildings have been darkened by the rains, as the valley receives more cloud. A weather system surrounds Cochabamba within the movement of vapour.

Moments in Time.
Storm Notes. Altiplano.

The sky darkens, spreading across the horizon and falling to the level of the plain. We enter an immense rain storm. Suddenly the altiplano transforms, surfaces darken and the aura of distance is gone. The mass of the mountains fade as the temperature drops and lightning breaks the wall of convecting air that is now around us. A brown sea has now formed where fields had previously stretched beneath the afternoon sun. Rivulets snake across the vast surface to find a course to carry their waters to the lower levels. A saturated sea lies beneath the churning and chanting of thunder. To the north lightness signals the edge of the storm, revealing the jagged peaks of the mountains, as hail dances on the front screen of the bus and ice collects on the exhausted wipers, only to shear off to the roadside.

Moments in Time.
The Place of Storms. Lake Titicaca.

The wave energy of the shore at an altitude of twelve thousand feet is a unique phenomenon, and as the bus approaches Copacabana and the expanse of the lake, so the reality of this elevated, inland sea begins to unfold. Placed between parallel cordillera of the Andes, Lake Titcaca is a place of storms. Covecting air builds upon the Altiplano to become trapped between these mountains.

It is here that the drama of the water cycle is played out with a thunderous regularity. Winds from the south meet the warm air of the northern tropics, activating cyclonic energy. In this elevated place it is a process that was to become the very foundation of the Inca faith, based as it was upon an earth deity. It was also a process that would dominate my days in Copacabana.

28.12.2005. 20.00. hours.
During the final hours of daylight just such a storm can be seen building to the west and stretching north into the mountains of Peru. Drifting towards the cool waters of the lake it now generates a silent display of lightning. Each pulse exposes an entire panorama of silver blue light, sending lightning to ground far across the waters and parading the outline of islands against the electric screen beyond. Earlier, as I drew by the lakeside I noticed how the towering clouds appeared to rise steeply from the water surface.

29.12. 2005. 20.00 hours. Lightning fills the sky to the south. Gazing from the window I see coaches adorned with flowers, freshly blessed from their earlier visit to the cathedral, departing from the shore as the first thunder rolls across the water to the lights of Copacabana. 21.00 hours. The storm is now concentrated to the north and reduced by distance, as the lightning bolts lay low to the far horizon, sending their charges arching over the entire length of the lake, to the rhythm of waves breaking along the shoreline.

30.12. 2005. 21.00 hours. Evening, and the ritual of the electric storm, as both lightning and thunder fill the night air, sending light across the lake waters and over the soft contours of the Inca islands of the sun and moon. With the night comes persistent rain, plunging Copacabana into a black deluge. Streets fill with torrents, flowing down to the lake and lifting manhole covers to cut deep channels across the dark sands of the shore.

Moments in Time.
Mountain Notes. Chacaltaya.

The taxi follows the rough track to the mountains, departing La Paz and passing through El Alto to rise beyond the barren surface of terrain that encircles the urban area. Wild dogs and llama graze and scamper by the roadside, as we gradually rise high into the mountains amid snow patches and the foothills of Huayna Potosí. The high peaks are seen fleetingly as cloud layers drift across the glaciated slopes. As we approach Chacaltaya it is clear that much of the snow and ice is in a state of melt and that the glacier is now fragmenting into isolated snow fields. I leave the taxi as the road ends abruptly in the remnants of a rock fall. Snow melt flows across the rock surfaces, making traverse a difficult and lengthy process. I enter a wooden shelter at the base of the final slope that leads to the peak. On the walls old photographs fade beneath discoloured perspex. The photographs tell the story of retreating ice over a period of sixty years and as I gaze through the small window towards the glacier it is clear that it has entered the final phase of retreat. Leaving the shelter of the hut I ascend the gentle slope to the peak and sit awhile to observe the surrounding mountains. The heights of Huayna Potosí to the north display glaciers that are intact on the southern slopes, though even these show crevassing and the failing contours of the snowfields. The landscape before me is in transition. Climate change will alter the erosional emphasis, whereby the force of frost and ice will be superseded by wind and rain. Here, in the high Andes, the grip of ice is loosening its hold upon the mountain slopes.

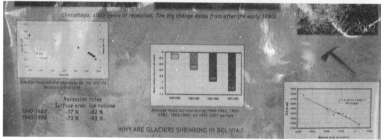

Chacaltaya: sixty years of recession. The big change dates from after the early 1980s.

WHY ARE GLACIERS SHRINKING IN BOLIVIA?

Moments in Time.
Tiwanaku.*

As I journey back to La Paz I decide to linger awhile upon the open lands of the altiplano and I approach the ruins of Tiwanaku, hardly visible above the barren surface of the fields. It is early evening and the light is fading. Climate change had brought an end to this society, as it had for the Moche and the peoples of the Inca period. Now it lies before me like an open page of history, exposed to the physical potency of the land processes that it had held so sacred. The irregular outline of a man-made surface can still be seen in the half light, transitional now between the peopled world and the timeless surface of the earth.

Tiwanaku society had declined after 1000 AD, from its position as the focus of a culture of sacred geography. With its alignment to the mountain deities of Illampu, Sajama and Illumani, it had enjoyed a close proximity to the waters of Lake Titicaca. Dominant within the spread of ruins before me I can see Akapana, a man-made hill constructed with both internal and external water pipes. Today the people of Bolivia still look to the mountains for their water, but with the disappearance of the glaciers the populated areas around La Paz face an uncertain future. It is a future made more hazardous by the cycle of drought of recent times.

Turning from the grey outline of the ruins, I walk along a straight track into the small town to be greeted by the combined sounds of a brass band and pipes. Vehicles arranged in front of the church are blessed with flowers and a wedding party emerges from a dark interior to a blizzard of confetti. Winds carry the coloured paper high into the night sky, away from the lights of the town to the fields and ruins that lay within the silent darkness of the past.

*Collage. 2008.

The Tablelands. Newfoundland.

Sketch the Second.

Newfoundland, a perpetual dream from that first day. That momentous day when the boats ground the shingle and waves turned the surf under a fresh sky, when the clouds raced to the west lifting from the great sea. That was the dream of Newfoundland. When the gates of the north were wide open and whales swam within the southern drift of ice, held in a geography where the systems of the earth conspired together and men stood on a distant shore, aware of their moment within those natural laws.

Woody Point. Newfoundland. 2006.

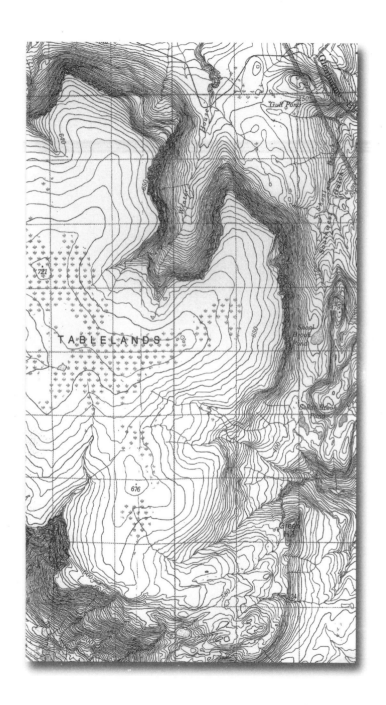

The Tropospheric World

The Newfoundland Tablelands - 2006.
Elevation. 2500'
Latitude. 50 degrees north.

Early morning fog was all but
burnt away, as the top of the
tablelands appeared from the haze.

Shapes bruised their way through
the fog, with the tops floating upon
a cushion of white air.

26.6.2006. 9.00 hours.

As I walk down to Water Street, within the small community of Woody Point, the tablelands gradually emerge from the fog of early morning. These rock massifs have come to dominate my time in Newfoundland. Their remoteness, both physical and mental, have created a release from the languor of lowland terrain and estuary. Water Street, lined with weathered surfaces of old boarding, is now permeated with the smell of salt water. Fresh breezes blow from the Gulf of St Lawrence, as I track along the shoreline, taking in details of stone and rock. The shore is littered with the unfamiliar shapes of moose and caribou bone fragments, too heavy for sea creatures or those of the air. Old rock brought back from some ancient holocene seabed now co-exists with the flotsam of small craft. Along the back shore a line of partly decimated huts in a state of collapse are in the process of slow burial by the accumulation of pebbles that have been shifted and sorted upon these shores, wearing them flat and smooth like an old coinage.

In the freshening breeze I backtrack towards the Granite Coffee Shop that stands at the eastern end of the street. The wood-built structure overlooks the broad inlet where granite ballast was discarded during the second world war by the Royal Navy, so that the ships could take on fresh fish. The coffee shop has become an automatic first stop during my stay at Woody Point, before venturing into the glaciated uplands of the Gros Morne region or tracking the coast of the south arm of Bonne Bay to the open waters of the St Lawrence. Rose brings my coffee and standard custard creams to the window seat: the coffee shop is a place for casual conversation and Rose is full of local knowledge. During my visits I have heard recollections of weather changes and the transition of the seasons. This year the snows of the winter had no foundation, in that the ground had not been frosted and frozen and subsequently the surface covering soon thawed and the snow was gone. Grave digging was easy within the soft ground.

Winters were clearly harder in past years when the whole south arm of the bay would freeze over, with the exception of the more active waters of Norris Point. Humpback whales could be heard coming in with the caplin, moving slowly along the ocean floor beneath the ice. These hard winters had enabled shoreline communities to have greater contact with each other; traversing the ice was a whole lot quicker than the long journey around the entire bay. With the ice firmly in, people would sometimes move home, placing their wooden houses on large sledges and logs, pulling them across the ice to fix them to a new piece of land and a new view.

With a lull in the conversation I gaze out of the window and watch the water surface for any signs of incoming whales or the rapid flight of bald headed eagles. I look at the mist rising from the cool surface. High above the tree-line the tablelands are clear as they warm within the early morning sun. Snow patches have steadily diminished during my stay, but can still be seen in the necklace of combes that line the upper slopes of the massif. Occasionally, caribou can be seen rolling in the snow in an attempt to gain relief from the incessant aggravation of midges. Soon the sun will be beating down on that ancient ocean floor and throughout the day will be humming off from the crystalline surface.

Down here by the waterside an elderly shoreman is preparing his boat for the day; beyond him the water surface is disturbed by breezes from the gulf. A flying boat passes noisily overhead and flies towards the tablelands. As it nears the high massif it seems to scale down and appears moth-like against the rock-faces beyond, as it slowly tracks to the east across the combes. My observations from the window are disturbed as a group of fishermen enter and become animated by conversation about the uncertainty of the caplin fishing grounds. Talk of the caplin remind me of my recent walk to Trent River Bay, when beyond the chaotic spread of old huts and homesteads I came to a symmetrical bay and an incoming tide of dead caplin. The air had filled with the richness of decay and I had walked along the waterline where the small fish had accumulated, each perfect with gills and mouths open in their dying gasp of air, some bent upwards as if to get that last taste of life. Upon the upper reaches of the beach, dry wood smoothed by its long journey within the waters of the St Lawrence, lay bleached to a bone grey. My attention returns to the fishermen as they bewail the lack of codfish within the waters of Newfoundland, stating that the waters of Nova Scotia are now the prime fishing grounds for this prize catch. Their conversation becomes more animated as they talk their way along the coasts, south to Vermont and north to the icy waters of Labrador. Fleetingly, their talk covers the vast coastlines of the salt zone, with an ease of familiarity with those shores and fishing grounds and an innate sense of the contours of the seabed. This knowledge of vastness fills the air and falls upon the surfaces of table and floor within the small room. As they talk of the absence of whale, Rose enters the conversation with further reminiscence of past seasons and gradually the act of recollection slows to a reflective silence.

I return to my window gazing and contemplate the day ahead on the Tableland, running through a list of essentials. Although the massif only rises to less than three thousand feet, weather changes can be rapid and exposure extreme. With the movement of low cloud orientation becomes impossible upon what is effectively a featureless surface of disintegrating rock.

As I depart from the coffee shop heat is beginning to rise from the hard surfaces and the fog has all but burnt off, only entering the bay now in small patches. I begin a slow walk, conscious of keeping heat exhaustion and dehydration to a minimum. By 11.00 hours I am at the base of the massif close to the eastern flank. Rising slowly, I rest near the lip of a combe amid the urgent sounds of snow melt.

Strange is the mix of exhaustion and high altitude as I enter the symmetry of the combe. Thought processes become disorientated as the effect of inverted gravity within these upper slopes draws me on to the higher surfaces. On the level plateau of the Tablelands I sit in the cooling breeze as the exertion of the climb falls away, and consider points from which to sketch: I begin to notice the more distinctive rock clusters where the larger tilted blocks break the line of horizon, aware that in all directions the level surface extends to an edge and that beyond those points clouds are rising from the lower terrain.

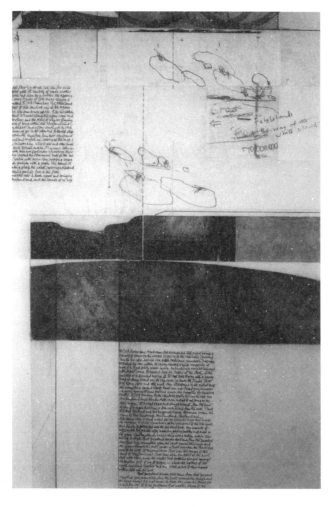

Photomontage. 2006.

Far back in geological time these rocks were forming upon an ocean floor, tempered by contact with the mantle of the planet. Their rise over this vast time had placed them above the immediate effects of the last glacial advance. They were within a parallel world that would only look down upon the chaotic processes of advance and retreat that were to be enacted beneath them. In these episodes they were a mere witness in a periglacial world where frost erupted to produce mounds of finely broken rock. A patterned crockery arranged by the forces of ice. As the surface had exhaled and inhaled beneath the skies of the Pleistocene, so the rock colourisation had altered to a light grey from the oxidised browns of the lower layers.

No bone or feather lies here and but for the juniper that grips its skeletal hand to the rock; no life exists on these surfaces or in the air above.

This is a place apart, in the way of the white cloud, and I am enveloped in a silence as I begin to clamber over the rocky terrain to my first sketching point that takes the form of a slight rise of larger rocks. Sounds produced from walking upon stone fragments and brittle juniper seem magnified.

13.00 hours. As I break off from sketching I look northwards to the heights of Gros Morne that dominate this upland region of western Newfoundland. A solitary cloud moves above the waters of Bonne Bay and travels slowly south towards me, fragmenting and transforming as it sails over the grey water surface and along the wooded slopes below. Pressed against the lower ramparts of the Tableland it is forced to rise and fade into the cool upper air. I move to another sketching point, the third from which my panoramic drawing will be composed and once again am aware of the sounds that revolve around my movements. The drawing points form a large circle around a central rock mass where my red rucksack forms the only colour within this grey infinity. The vocabulary of sounds continues as winds blow across the top of my open water container producing a harmonic that accompanies the turning pages of my notebook. I sit upon a large block of peroditite; the processes of denudation have produced fine fragments of rock that have accumulated in the deep fissures and joints of the rock surface.

I reflect upon the length of time of these processes, arranged as they are by the force of gravity. Completing the fourth drawing I stand to restore the circulation within my legs and decide to make a descent into the glacial trough that is known as Winter House.

15.00 hours. Entering the steep cut I follow the line of contour across the scree slope, working my way gradually down towards Winter House brook. The flanks of the combe are steep and indicate the power of downcutting produced by ice

movement. Winds of the Pleistocene would have carried drifting snow from the exposed tableland to accumulate in the valley. Such quantities of snow would provide for a considerable glacier capable of cutting the incised hollow in which I now walk. I follow the stream that flows rapidly from the remaining snow patches and find a suitable place from which to draw. The sky is now partly overcast, but the aerial dome above me within this amphitheatre of rock gives a sense of rounded containment and I sit as if within a vast sphere. Looking through my binoculars I locate a levee of rock from where I can sketch the upper slopes of the combe and I climb again towards a large snow patch. From where I sit I can see the symmetry of the whole of Winter House; the rim of crags gives way to a broad skirt of loose scree that angles down to the valley floor.

18.00 hours. In fading light I make my way out of the combe. The weather is deteriorating and the rock details that I have been sketching are now part of a dark and indistinct gloom. As I descend so the sounds of meltwater increase and I am forced to ford a number of streams before leaving the valley.

Within the last light of the day clouds are now entering the area of Bonne Bay; low clouds force their path within the turmoil of constant transition. A white cloud, full and convecting with the weight of suspended crystals, imperceptibly cushions the high tableland and falls below the line of vision.

Part Two
The Hercynian Forest

Finland and the Baltic Sea

Sketch the Third.

A glimpse of that
underworld, as the fox
emerges from the dark
shadows of the Hercynian forest.
Timeless, that step,
silently moving across
the scene before me.
Left to right between
the black verticals.

Kokar. Aland Archipelago. 2007.

Dark Northland,
the man-eating, the
fellow drowning place.

Extract from the *Kalevala*
National Epic of Finland.

Sketch the Fourth.

North,
beyond those dark, threatening
forests of Grunewald,
into the polar light
of the magnetic field
and the uncertain world
of shifting force.

Tricking the mast
as vessels follow
the converging lines.

The Gulf of Bothnia. 2007.

I am where all light is mute
with a bellowing like the ocean.
Turbulent in a storm of warring winds.
The hurricane of Hell in perpetual motion.

Dante. *The Inferno*

And deer in terror struggling through the new
    spread
Fields of a world-wide flood.

The Odes of Horace

The Hercynian Forest.

The Baltic Sea. Aland. 2007.
Elevation. Sea level.
Latitude. 60 degrees north.

5.2.2007. From high altitude I look down upon an apparent snowscape of billowing cloud; still, suspended and frozen, only to be transformed into a descent of flakes. From my window seat I can see other planes, silent and rapid, skimming over some other terrain, dwarfed by the immense alien world of upper sky. Above the coast of Northern Germany sea describes the eastern littoral zone of the North Sea. East, and the first white crazed outlines of ice within a geometry of fields, obscured occasionally by the path of the clouds. Eventually, over the dark waters of the Baltic and a negative print composed of white roofs and fields and the black arteries of road and rail track define the southern coastal area of Finland, held now within the iron grip of winter.

17.00 hours. On the road to Turku, within a fading light held by the reflective surface of snow. Beyond the wayside heaps of broken ice and dull snow, a gloaming of tree and field await the step of the hunter.

21.00 hours. Within the lounge of the seaport Hotel I look across a frozen street, and beyond the shuffling pedestrians stands the high silhouette of a Baltic ferry,

6.2.2007. An early departure for Marieheim and Kokar within the Aland archipelago: the numerous islands mark the meeting of the waters from the Gulf of Bothnia and the Baltic Sea. Despite the apparent cold I am told that recent winters have produced above average temperatures. February usually sees the freezing of the Gulf of Finland and Bothnia, with a grip of ice that spreads west into Baltic Sea. Only icebreakers would keep the sea lanes open for the ferries that serve the ports from Stockholm to St Petersburg. The degradation of the Baltic environment continues relentlessly with pollution from Poland and Germany as well as the increase in ferries from the east, to the extent that rocky areas that skirt the islands have an extensive yellow deposit upon them.

Fishing grounds have been depleted, over-fished and decimated by the surrounding countries. Algae bloom and wither, sinking to the seabed to produce a foul-smelling water that poisons the sealife. The late arrival of ice in recent years has also affected communities of the small islands that are now becoming more isolated as ice no longer allows the interchange across the frozen channels.

9.00 hours. From the ship I look across a small bay. Vapour rises from the icy waters and filters through the dark outlines of conifers that line the water's edge. A three-quarter moon gives light within the cloudless early morning sky, as seabirds gather upon the frozen surface of the sea where a thin film of meltwater gives off

vapour into the cold air. The ship makes its way through the deep water channels, passing wooded slopes as the sun begins to disperse the drift of the mist. Occasionally, outlines of rock or tree break through the white air, but for much of the journey a thick sea fog fills the air above the waters and islands. During the voyage I escape the ballroom dancing and the karaoke of my fellow passengers with brief visits to the open deck.

On the ice encrusted metal steps I pause to study a large navigational chart of the sea area. The Aland archipelago and the southern island of Kokar are clearly marked amid a frenzy of shipping lanes, lighthouses, beacons and fathom readings. Hundreds of small islands or skerries fill the waters off the south-west coast of Finland, each with its own distinctive signalling code.

14.00 hours. At Marieheim I transfer from the larger ship to a local ferry service for the final part of the journey to Kokar. The small vessel slowly makes its way out to the open waters through the ice that has formed within the shelter of the bay.

The landscape of the islands has been dictated by the retreat of the glaciers, which ground the hard rapakin granite down to the low contours of today. The glaciers went north over six thousand years ago when Aland consisted of only a few islands. As the ice departed so the land rose, creating thousands of small skerries. The land still rises by five centimetres a year, temporarily defying the onset of rising sea levels. The exposed outcrops of red granite display the footprint left by the ice in the form of deep striations produced as the frozen shadow left the land.

Occasionally the great circulation of waters from the Baltic Sea produce huge swell waves that break unexpectedly over the low lying islands of Aland. This, and the rising incidence of storms, are the only elements that cleanse the polluted waters.

7.2.2007. Gastham Inlet. Kokar. 2.30 hours.
My first glimpse beyond the window of a landscape bathed in moonlight, showing a silver land of snow surface and lunar shadow. A still and frozen scene awaiting the daylight. That gaze upon a silent world remained with me during the early days at Gastham. The narrow waters of the inlet stayed hard frozen, and at the seaward entrance the great push of ice from the Baltic Sea created a fractured field of broken sheets that stabbed their sharp edges into the frozen air. Sounds rose from the white surface as the constricted ice manoeuvred its bulk along the shorelines and wooden jetties.

8.00 hours. I attempt drawing within the cold air but am unable to handle the sharp contours and forms before me: the air, too clear, is devoid of the depth I need and I am forced to leave the paper on the slatted wooden surface, weighed down with my bag to prevent it lifting in the breeze. Walking along the jetties, sounds continue to fire across the surface as it adjusts to the changing temperature. Loud pistol like sounds suggest a possible seal movement from beneath the ice and as I walk on an extended jetty to the centre of the inlet, trapped ice beneath the planking explodes into a fractured spray of crystals that slide along the surface.

Those early days enabled me to plan out my stay at this lonely post. Observations from the comfort of the window seat established a working relationship with the dimensions of the inlet, while the local radio station kept me aware of the outer geography of these waters. The voice had crackled into what sounded like the Finnish equivalent of the shipping news. My imagination had spun around the sea lanes as the speaker listed the various waters.

'Bornholm, steady, strong to gale force, good. Gotland, steady, force six to seven, three hundred metres. Gulf of Bothnia, rising, force seven to eight, fair. Gulf of Finland, rising, gale force nine imminent, good.'

And so it went on, and I became aware of my position of isolation upon this small island within a navigational chart, lost amid the arrowing lines and beacons.

9.2.2007. 8.00 hours. The cold weather continues and I look out upon a frozen inlet. The sky displays breaks within the cloud mass as beams of sunlight catch the broad white surfaces of the upper massifs. There are occasional flurries of snow. I decide to spend the day on the west coast of the Hamno area. With a slight wind and good visibility I should be able to study the line of offshore skerries and observe the seabird nesting areas. Kokar covers a small acreage compared to some of the islands within the archipelago, but it is a dispersed land area and journey times can be surprisingly long. However, by 11.00 hours I begin to make my way through thin woodland to the coast of Hamno and in the gentle snowfall I follow the track of a fox which leads me to a small cove.

The cove is frozen within the grip of ice and high pitched sounds are rising above the small perimeter. I decide to record the sounds of moving ice, whilst observing the flight of a black guillemot and a large swan beyond the frozen inlet. Tidal movement rocks the plate of ice that is lodged within the cove, producing ah elaborate symphony of high pitched sound. This gradual inhalation and exhalation comes from the depths of the Baltic, from beyond the outer islands.

Making my way gradually to the north along the rock-strewn coast, I can see these skerries clearly, with their apron of ice traced along the darkness of their foreshores. The waters within the Baltic and Finland seas freeze rapidly and the sea ice is frequently seen clinging to the rock surfaces high above the water level. Distant swell to the west sends a surge of water over these low lying islands, carrying the sea ice above the tidal range. Within the rock massifs I uncover the bones and feathers of a large seabird. My usual practice of collecting specimens in the field has been impossible, due to the thin blanket of snow, and pure chance has caused my foot to dislodge the discoloured bones. The kill was probably that of a sea eagle and the array of bones suggests that the prey was a large gull or gannet. Little remains of the carcass and I use the wing bone as a tool and scrap away the ice and snow to retrace the last moments of life. The struggle revealed indicates that it took place some time ago, probably in late summer before the freezing of the ground.

Tracking along the coast I come to a broad bay with a foreshore of large boulders. It is a difficult coastline of slippery surfaces. Offshore I can see a line of skerries including Stenskar, Pattarkar and Ostra Rodgrund, while to the north the large island of Kanskar stands high within the icy waters. I sit upon a small promontory, which extends into the frozen waters of the bay and listen to the strained pitch of ice crystals. Out at sea, beyond the skerries, I can see a group of eider ducks and a number of cormorants as they feed within the choppy waters, Snow falls steadily and sea eagles glide overhead towards land, only to fade in the flurries.

14.00 hours. As the snow begins to ease and sunlight warms the shore, I select a suitable position for drawing. Two hours of clear daylight in dry conditions should

be enough to achieve the outlines of the drawing and I set to work, focusing upon the details of a large granite rock mass.

10.2.2007. 8.00 hours. Daybreak, and from clear skies the sun now casts its low light across frozen surfaces. There is no movement at all and the tall reeds rising from the ice appear as if caught within an old photographic still. Numb ice chokes the inlet. From the frozen shores I head inland over a terrain of rock massifs and wooded slopes of conifers that form a badlands within the heart of the island.

Stumbling through the steep wooded heights I emerge into the warm light of a clearing. I look west and see two large red deer, fleetingly,

as they scamper, with cloven hoof upon hard granite,
ringing
into the dark hercynian shadows.

I reach Hamn Inlet, low-lying and serene in the morning sun, with the edge of frozen water midway to the skerries. Ice surfaces glisten like granulated glass. At sea the sound of a small vessel rises and falls as it passes behind the individual islands, eventually sending a white wave pulsing towards me through the thin floe ice.

I make my way around the rocky headland of Svaleholm and enter the large inlet of Gastham. Ice fills the entire area, held firm and still. Fox trails lead from the cover of rock and cross the ice; a strange track of parallel prints suggest a steady and measured pace of a creature aware of the strength of the ice beneath.

I am held within a silent, slow film that fades occasionally with the sound of ice. Here, along the frozen shores of Gastham, the mechanical movement of crystals fracture the air above the drum of surface tension.

Following those brief and unexpected glimpses of the snowprints, my awareness of the presence of this other being was growing. A relationship translated solely by an imprint in snow, a fleeting language conditioned by the delicate surface of frozen water. In my mind an image was forming, steadily taking shape, as if held within the dark room of the photographer. There was a comfort in these thoughts. Within the forest there was another mind that was considering the spatial world of trees, making decisions of track and observing the 'way'. An intelligence wholly appropriate to this place was increasingly permeating my thoughts

It was a relationship built upon a catalogue of momentary decisions that formed order, like the laying down of snow.

15.30 hours. I retrace my way back to Gastham, pausing to prise pieces of discarded flotsam from the frozen shore, but the ice will not release its hold. As I rise over the smooth upper rock surfaces, so the step of the fox reappears in the white surface. As the light fades I can make out the tracks made in the early hours; warmth of the day's sun has enlarged the imprints in a slow melt, but they are still clear.

As the days pass so the trails increase, some partly buried, some sharp and clear, until the foxprints form a lattice of hunting paths. With each new trail discovered so our bond became stronger, such that with the first sighting upon the granites of Nabban high above the frozen surface of the inlet, this simply formed another chapter in this growing relationship. I followed his movements through my binoculars. His russet colouring grew darker in the fading light and his movements became silhouetted against the backdrop of snow as he stepped soundlessly between the black verticals of the tree cover.

12.2.2007. 8.30 hours. Sunrise, and a gentle early light picks out the fracture lines forming across the ice within Gastham. The pressure from the shifting waters to the west has eventually proved too much for the tight surface of ice. Instinctively I look across the inlet to the opposite shore and pick up the slow movements of the fox within the trees. The effortless lope is occasionally disturbed as the fox stops to sniff the air. Before me this wild creature is completely at ease within the terrain of rock and woodland. Following the movements, I become aware that this reflective and intelligent creature has appeared, as if from some historic backdrop.

As a child growing up in London, part of my education had involved visits to the great museums and art galleries which included the National Gallery. In the days before the gallery extended into the Sainsbury Wing, Renaissance art was encountered almost immediately on entrance into the main hall. Confronting Piero di Cosimo's painting of a 'Satyr Mourning over a Nymph' was unavoidable. That confrontation had opened a vision onto a somewhat dysfunctional world of satyrs, within an expansive and mysterious landscape, inhabited by an element of animal intelligence.

The significance of the painting is still being played out as I pursue a path within a world of natural disorder and chaos. This path, both singular and in solitude, enters into the painting. I have always wanted to walk into that landscape; thin in oxygen, full of wonderful creatures and out of step with time. Close examination of the painting focuses upon the inflection of the dog's head, indicating movement and a correction by the artist that still ghosts through the centuries establishing the dog in the central role, elevating the animal to dominate over the drama of the scene. In this the painting is a statement of animal intelligence, both wild and beyond the human experience.

I continue to follow the movements of the fox with its slow step playing out a scene within the song of the dark forest. 11.00 hours. I track out to Gronvik Bay and the extreme west of Kokar. It is a maritime environment facing the broad waters of the Baltic. The sea is bringing much brash ice into the bay, and with it the noise from the collision of loose ice and rock. It is a white sea, within a crucible of light, as the sun reaches its highest point.

My fellowship with the fox continues and I follow a trail down to the shore that takes me between large rock masses, thus avoiding the steep inclines and impenetrable depths of woodland. I reach the safety of a rock shore and begin to record the cacophonous sound of incoming ice. I manage to achieve two hours of work, and intersperse recording by sheltering within an abandoned hut, before backtracking out from the bay along the fox trail, still visible in the loaming of early evening.

14.2.2007. 8.00 hours. I wake to the return of the pure surface of snow. Before me a blizzard fills the inlet of Gastham. The nearby rock detail is lost beneath a thick even covering, while visibility has reduced the far shore to a light grey blur of trees and rock. The sastrugi has been buried by the falling snow and with it, the trail of the fox.

The combination of frozen sea and heavy snow signals the time when the isolated communities of the archipelago would become as one. The severe conditions of past winters provided an ice bridge, linking island to island and skerry to skerry. But now as I look out beyond the frozen surface I can just make out the active waters through the curtain of snow. Skerries are now more isolated, less frequently disturbed by the foot of man. Gradually their surfaces will become wild, littered with bone and feather. No longer part of the white highway of winter, they have become an untrodden land of moss growth and the colonisation of wind blown seed.

11.00 hours. Within this brief glimpse of winter I decide to head to the Hamno coast, and retrace my steps along the coast that leads south towards Langskar inlet. Before confronting the granite coast I enter the Franciscan Chapel, situated high upon the northern rocks. Hamno is almost a separate island from Kokar, attached by a slender cord of rock debris, lying deep beneath the freshly fallen snow. Within the chapel simple wooden cases of archaeological finds are arranged along the inner walls, and contain fine styli of bone and delicate vessels of pottery. Across the old stone flooring the humble footprint of the original chapel is all that remains. Snow continues to fall as 1 head south to the inlet. By the time I reach Langskar it is held deep within the snow. I sit upon the rock boulders of the shoreline, as the ebb and flow from the open sea pulses through the ice layers. I record the ice sounds; acoustics are good within the inlet with its narrowing of rock surfaces and backdrop of dense woodland. Occasionally the sound of a swan call enters from the sea. There is little wind and an additional surge of water enters the perimeter of the inlet, sounding its way through the ice towards the shallow shore where I sit. 13.00 hours. A sudden fall of temperature grips the still air and within the sky I can see the grey outlines of a cold front as it is dragged overhead. An immense cyclonic system slowly drifts from the west, lifting breezes from the surface of the Baltic Sea. Dark clouds move silently over the white land; the snow cover is complete, producing a decibel beyond the sound that is silence. The world turns like a slow memory wheel.

Over the remaining days the weather continued to fluctuate. Mornings revealed the return of the fox, the trails discernible across the still frozen waters of Gastham. My state of isolation within the islands had led to a closer link with the ways of the wild creature and a passing of time had allowed me to enter into its rhythm and step. Familiarity with contour and the memory of that first moonlit glimpse of the scene from the window enabled me to consider the surfaces now lying deep beneath the snow cover. Within a short passage of time I had become aware of the element of change being enacted before me. Whether it heralded a denunciation of the earth's steady state or indeed a change of climate was not clear. That a pulse of change within the snow-covered surfaces was rising from the earth's inner core. These thoughts thread through history, audible to none but the wild creature within the world of a Renaissance artist.

15.2.2007. 10.30 hours. I set off towards Hakosnas at the southern tip of Kokar, where land gives way to a sea of rocky islands and skerries. Walking through the primeval woodland of the northern forests, footprints deep in the snow from fox and elk cross the path and fade into the distance of field and tree cover. The entire bay of Hakosstrommen is frozen and the skerries of Arpskar, Agg-kuggskar and Utterskar are all merged into what appears as an expansive coastline. Even as I sketch, however, I notice that the surface of the ice is changing; dark patches are spreading and forming small polynas, as the sudden temperature changes impact upon the white sheet before me.

The sketch finished, I continue walking to maintain body temperature and make for the southern point. Climbing down to an indistinct shore of ice and snow I sit and ponder upon a small hut, situated high upon the spine of Aspskar skerry, some two kilometres from the shore.

It is placed such that it has a vast panorama of the Baltic to seaward and the sheltered waters of the inner skerries to landward. One hundred and eighty degrees of sky arcs over its grey roof. On a clear day the sun would work its warm touch gradually around three of the white walls. Today, however, it stands discarded and silent, but for the four winds. A symbol of solitude and isolation, this place anchors the fallacy of a dream to a set point upon a granite outcrop. Thoughts within this abandoned hinterland become distracted, as I notice a wandering line of prints trailing across the frozen waters to one of the larger skerries.

19.2.2007. My remaining days on Kokar have seen the return to the comparative warmth of recent winters, and as in many other latitudes, so also a slipping away of the seasons. Amid it all the thinning of the ice, draining away to the north, emptying as if from a great sink. 11.00 hours. I head for Skorkiappen and the promontory of Ravaska, which juts out into the deep waters to the south-west. Despite the rise in temperature the sea surface is still frozen, visible beneath a thin layer of meltwater. From the shelter of discarded huts I venture out onto the low skerries and collect flotsam, caught here within an easterly drift. Heading back to Karlby and the low-lying central area of Kokar, I am met by a blizzard, which immediately transforms the island back into the abyss that is winter. For now, the snow returns, falling so hard that I can hear the flakes hitting my waterproof clothing and the nearby hard surfaces. Eventually, I reach Karlby amid the fading visibility of the maelstrom.

It is some time since I departed Kokar. Much has come to rest within my memory, but there lingers an unease of the slow change being enacted within these islands. That gradual alteration of island geography, responding to the forces of land and sea levels, is almost unwitnessed. The rising of an unburdened land, within the uncertainty of sea levels, forms a precarious relationship that can alter in rapid time.

The initiatives of Johan Mansson in the 1640s that established the practice of keeping sea books and charts as well as the placing of buoys and lights upon the many shoals is as relevant now as in those early days of navigation.

During my stay on Kokar evenings were sometimes spent making my way along the hazardous shores of Gastham inlet until I reached the broad span of the open sea. From those frozen shores I could see the lights and beacons of the Baltic to the west and those of the Bothnia Sea to the north.

An electric geography flickering and pulsing through the dark hours, producing a carpet of light that contained a geometry of the night sky. Bengtskar light high upon its granite platform illuminating the skerries of the Marieheim Straits, and Lagskar, distant and all but lost within the foreign waters of the north.

Part Three
Ice Bears and Time Lines

Svalbard, Norway

Sketch the Fifth.

'Peary took 13 readings to ascertain his position: he built a semi-circular poachers shelter of ice, facing south in which he placed an artificial horizon comprising a wooden trough, filled to the brim with mercury and resting on a mat of fur, lest it freeze on contact with the ice. The trough pointed lengthways to the south and on its sides were balanced two glass panes, joined at the top to form an inverted V, which protected the mercury from the wind and from snow or crystals in the atmosphere. He threw down a fur at one end of the trough to insulate him from the cold and to block refraction from the ice, while he lay down and aimed his sextant at the sun's reflection in the mercury. The result was 89° 57' N.

Assuming he was wrong by at least 10 miles he continued north until he passed the pole and headed south, whereupon he marched back to where he guessed the pole to be.'

Robert Peary. 1909. Adaptation from 90 North by Fergus Fleming.

Sketch the Sixth.

The year is 1585 and a small group
huddle together on the ice, intent
upon their music.

Small dark figures within a white
infinity and the notes dispatched into
the frozen auditorium that is the Arctic,
skidding along the ice like the ivory
of piano keys.

And the inuit,
what do they make of it all?

This performance,
so far removed from
the dull moan of survival.

Adaptation from an account by John Davies in 1585, near to Baffin Island, as he
worked on ice conditions, weather and terrain.

Ice Bears and Time Lines.

Ny-Alesund Research Base 2006.
Svalbard Archipeligo.
Elevation. Sea Level.
Latitude. 79 degrees north.

Looking north from high altitude, above a thick layer of cloud, a sharp white line describes the end of the world.

The journey north. 13.8.2006.
From the hotel window I look out upon a dark scene of green conifer and blue distant mountains. During the day overcast skies have been rising and turbulent, and from the televised forecast I see that an occluded front has provided the dense cloud cover stretching from the eastern shores of Britain to the mountains of Scandinavia. To the north an area of high pressure descends slowly upon the Arctic latitudes. I walk out into the last light of the day and sit awhile at the edge of the open fields. Conifers in the mid distance all but obscure the view of the distant hills that define the edge of Oslo. The silhouettes of the tree tops arrow into the cloud laden sky. There is a resinous smell within the air and the view before me holds a light, infused with dark green wash.

I consider the journey that will take me north. Three great strides, from Oslo to Tromso and on to Longyearbyen, before finally reaching the science base of Ny-Alesund, deep within the mountains and fiords of the northern archipelago of Svalbard.

14.8.2006. The flight to Tromso soon rises above the high cloud and enters the snowfields of convection. Occasionally I glimpse the terrain below held in the world of forest, mountain and glacier. There is a language of ice written in its retreat, through fjords and the shadow of mountains, leaving a puddled land of sporadic melt. The chaos of a receding force lies within the light of summer. From Tromso we pass the cloud hugging peaks and enter the high zone of the Arctic. Gradually the skies become clear and I look down onto a calm sea surface. Less than two hundred years ago these waters carried the hopes of sailors and explorers. Among them the Pomori sailors of Russia had travelled beneath thin white sails and had approached the fragmenting wall of the northern ice, only to be ship-wrecked and forced to survive for a six-year exile, before a chance rescue brought their remarkable story back to the lands of the south. For now, the blue, ice-free surface of the Barents Sea looks benign and accessible.

Eventually the first sighting of the archipelago. Glaciers extend over the land, broken by the mountain shadows of late afternoon. Steep ice falls and lines of collapse exist within the tortuous descent of ice and snow. Glaciers are blunted by their entry into the sea, sending channels of pulverised rock and mud into the open bays. As I look down upon this transforming landscape I am filled with the sensation of having caught up with time, where the hovering tracer rests upon the pulse of the planet.

Longyearbyen lies below low cloud as we transfer planes. From the small landing strip the surrounding mountains are partly shrouded, obscuring details of coal pits and slag, which scar the steep slopes. It is a drab and functional town with little charm. I pass through the security lounge and enter a small hangar, where luggage is being weighed before being loaded onto the twelve-seater plane. As we sit waiting for clearance to take off, I become distracted by a conversation between passengers across the narrow aisle. They talk of the seed store that is being established deep in the ice caverns and permafrost of Longyearbyen. This doomsday safety measure, containing all the variations of food supply, will be held securely for some future generation. It is a Noah's Ark of the modern age and it holds a strange and rather unsettling inevitability; I ponder this as the small plane begins to move slowly towards the windswept runway. With the acceleration of the twin engines we begin a rattling ascent into the cold air and bank steeply towards the northern horizon. Conversation above the sounds of the engines is only fragmentary and attention is soon turned to the glacial landscape beyond the small windows. Within the dark bays and inlets the white outlines of beluga whales can be seen drifting with the broken crockery of glacial ice. The land of northern Svalbard gives way to the meltwash plains and the crazed details of the tundra surface, but for much of the flight we pass slowly over the vast skin of old ice, discoloured by a grey covering of moraine.

14.8.2006. Ny-Alesund Research Base. 23.00 hours. Beyond the drawn curtains of my small study I am aware of the bright continuous light of a perpetual day. It is late in the season and the sun will barely touch the horizon. The sun will slowly fall, skimming the northern line, where its light will be diffused in low cloud above a surface of cold water. Lines of time seem suspended in the air, arrowing towards a point that is no land. A place of contrivance. Gradually, with the passing of the next few days, the sun will dip a little lower, eventually to fall below that hard northern line, sending a mute shadow across the land.

15.8.2006. 7.00 hours. I awake to the sounds of arctic tern and the occasional yelp from the direction of the dog enclosure, rising above the constant drone of the generator. Beyond the window an expanse of rough tundra is traversed by the elevated wires and pipes, held above the damaging effects of the frozen and twisting permafrost.

The day is to be spent on rifle training and I make my way past the low-lying wooden huts of the various research groups to the main building that serves as a refectory and administrative centre.

Following a brief outline of the essentials of defence against attack by polar bear, I am driven to the rifle range by Linda, who is to be my instructor for the day. Once upon the heights above Ny-Alesund I take in the broad panorama of Kongsfjorden, stretching southwards to the Ossian Sarsfjellet massif rising into the clear air above the glaciers. I am taken through the various components of the rifle and how to use it in the event of a confrontation with a bear, which I am told, is very rare. Linda patiently goes through the details; how a lead bullet will splay as it impacts on bone in order to maximise the damage inflicted, and to avoid aiming at the head of the bear, as it will be moving from side to side as it runs towards you. These details are rounded off with the bottom line that if the bear is within fifty metres it is probably too late anyway. Like a slow alarm bell drumming into my head I come to the realisation that to survive in this encounter I have to pre-empt every move of the bear and rely upon the comfort of distance. I fire the high velocity rifle and somehow manage to hit the target, but am appalled by the immense power of the weapon, as it jolts back into my shoulder.

These early thoughts on the dangers of the polar bear established a relationship between the hunter and the hunted that has stayed with me. Those early Pomori sailors would have been constantly aware of the white bear. Every moment of the day would see them alert and watchful, in the knowledge that death was a moment's space away. They would have stayed together all the time, as their meagre weapons, consisting of spears, would require the collective strength of the 'pack' rather than to rely upon a lone encounter. This obsession with survival would always be with them, throughout the six long years of exile, with its six long winters of darkness.

As Linda drives me back to base she continues her account of the way of the bear. In summer the thin bear is dangerous, as it is hungry and fast, and will actively hunt you once it has your scent. Bears have been observed to stand motionless in their hunting of seals for over an hour before making the sudden attack and kill. Linda teaches well and I am already scanning the open surface of the tundra for that potent white form. The hunted will carve a different understanding of the landscape, through the wide awareness of space, distance, surface and the obscure and unseen components of terrain. A lethal combination of rough surface, large rocks and hidden areas, so common amid glacial moraines, spreads out before me across the tundra to the shoreline. Looking now at these desolate surfaces, they seem to possess a potency of real danger. Within this crucible of life's struggle life itself may be extinguished like a light that fades and is gone.

16.00 hours. Returning to base I enter the boot room. It is distinctive and can be described as polar, possessing the collective smells of the field. Bone fragments, dry moss and frozen dung combine to produce a musky fragrance of something that was alive but is now dead. All life has gone from these things and the effect is not unpleasant. This is not a process of putrid decay, as that passing of life has left dry shell, brittle bone and discarded feathers. My shooting course completed, I decide to use the rest of the day in drawing from the landscape, and make for the elevated platform of the administrative building that serves the various science groups of Ny-Alesund. The upper rooms of the building are lined with photographs showing the departing air balloon of Roald Amundsen and other portraits of Nansen and Peary. I make my way to the open deck and sit in the cool evening air. I look south towards the prominent features of Kronebreen and the heights of Ossian Sarsfjellat. The retreating glaciers display the effects of pollution upon their surfaces, in the form of a grey bloom produced by industrial soot. The effect of this air pollutant is to reduce the reflectiveness of the sun's rays and subsequently the process of melt and retreat of the glaciers is accelerated. I commence drawing the surface of the nearby Midtre Lovenbreen glacier but the silence of Kongsfjorden is disturbed by the descent of the daily plane from Longyearbyen, as it makes its approach to the runway on the northern plateau lying beyond the huts of Ny-Alesund. I return to the drawing in the clear evening light. Silence has returned, but for the call of tern or skua and the low thunder of ice collapse from the distant glaciers.

20.00 hours. Walking along the tundra shoreline within the perimeter of the base, I pass the small, low-lying island of Prins Heinrichoya. The evening is clear with a cooling breeze entering Kongsfjorden from the north and creating a rough water surface around the prominent island of Blomstrandhalvoga, which stands high in the distant light. Arctic tern and skua, with high-pitched screams, follow the shoreline to my left as I walk southwards. Passing the small enclosure of the dog cemetery I can see wooden crosses with the old bridles hanging from them, as if they had brought their huskies here to rest until the brightness of a new day. I turn and head back towards the coloured outlines of the various buildings, each distinctive according to the different nationalities.

23.00 hours. I pull back the curtains to reveal bright sunlight, as it sends its long shadows across an endless day. Earth's axis and an angle out of alignment creates the phenomenon before me. The hands of my watch fast approach midnight, with its seamless entry into another day. These mysterious, suspended days coalesce into one as this northern light glances off the high latitudes of earth's northern arc.

16.8.2006. 8.00 hours. With the weather still set fair we decide to work within the same area of Kongsfjorden, where Roger, Yelena and Gordana will collect springtail* specimens from the cliffs and I shall sketch to the south, along the shoreline. With two rifles and boxes of science equipment we awkwardly manoeuvre into the heavy safety suits before clambering into the small boat that will take us the eight kilometres to the designated drop off point. The day is bright and warm with little breeze to disturb the water surface; the sea ice has virtually gone, with only the occasional small fragment drifting out of the fiord from the Conwaybreen and Kronebreen glaciers. From the drop off point I leave the others to work at the cliff face and track south-east along the shore towards the great glacier of Kronebreen. The glacier is unstable and from the shingle beach I can see water pouring from where the ice is calving into the fiord. Stepping across glacial outwash I notice two seals, as they break the still water surface close to the shoreline and reach instinctively for the rifle now firmly strapped across my shoulder. Within an hour I arrive at an abandoned hut in an advanced state of disintegration.

Equipment has been discarded, lamps are broken and tubes marked 'sucre' lie upon the chaos of stones around its perimeter. From the small windows I can see the snout of the glacier as it enters the waters of the fiord. Occasionally ice collapse thunders from the glacier. Within the debris of the hut I notice writing and markings, just visible upon the old wood surfaces. I decide to sit for a while within the hut, gazing through the small window beyond an old hurricane lamp that hangs from a rusty nail. Sounds of gull from a nearby cliff face and the incessant flow of glacial melt fill the air.

*Springtail. Common name for minute primitive six-legged arthropod.

Gradually I become immersed in a state of calm; the dimensions of this small shelter offer a form of comfort and I am held in a cool silence. Such moments rise beyond the state of silence and my awareness of the geography of this outpost is heightened. This sanctuary amid the harshness of mountain slope and ice is a place that I shall return to.

14.00 hours. As I step from the hut I am greeted by a crescendo of collapsed ice from the southern shore, which sends waves fanning out across the surface waters. I track back to the drop off point and disturb the arctic skuas, which immediately start to dive, and I am forced to hold the barrel of the rifle above my head to evade their attacks. Somewhere within the glacial moraine they will have placed their nesting areas and I have strayed too close to them. Eventually I reach the cliff face where the others are working at the springtail collection and begin to record the incessant sounds of gull coming from the crowded nesting areas. Kittiwake, herring gull, tern and skua all provide a continuous high pitch that magnifies against the crumbling rocks of the cliff. Elaborate nests have been constructed, giving the impression of an architecture of adobe, fixed firmly within the high overhangs above me. Arctic foxes climb over the lower scree, causing the gulls to become agitated. Overhead, adult birds lock within mid-air combat only to fall together before releasing each other at the last moment. As I stand and record the sounds I notice three foxes catch and kill a young kittiwake. It is one of many kills witnessed during the day, as the foxes climb among the huddle of the nests.

16.00 hours. The completion of my recording coincides with the end of the springtail collecting. Roger and I decide to walk back to base along the shores of Kongsfjorden, while Gordana and Yelena take the equipment and spare rifle in the boat. The shoreline is awash with meltwater as it fans out over the fine shingle. Occasionally we stop, exchanging the rifle and adjusting the loads on our backs while looking up to the constricted fields of ice held within the valleys. I sketch the upper combes that have been carved within the black volcanic rocks by the movement of ice, completing the drawing by superimposing an imaginary line indicating the maximum snow accumulation. It is clear that melt and retreat of the glacier has been taking place for some time, and that the present level sits deep within those earlier accumulations.

The dark body of the land, abandoned by the outgoing tide of ice, lies now like some huge subdued creature as we make our way within the thin light of evening.

17.8.2006. 7.00 hours. I wake to find Ny-Alesund enveloped within a low cloud. Only the stark outlines of the adjacent huts are visible. Beyond, the occasional fleck of snow patch on the lower slopes of Zeppelinfjellet breaks the wall of light grey moisture. Even the sound of the generator seems muted. Arctic foxes run between and beneath the wooden huts and a reindeer feeds on the meagre tundra vegetation that lies beyond the huts of the base. The reindeer of Spitsbergen are a smaller breed than their counterpart of Northern Russia, and are believed to have come on ice floes from the east. Stone Age hunters had seen reindeer go onto the ice and disappear over a frozen world towards what was believed to be a source of food, with their ability to smell land over huge distances. It is possible that migrations of inuit had followed these creatures, as they founded their sacred lands to the west and the north. This relationship of man and beast can still be appreciated, as both rely upon an intuitive sense of space in the ebb and flow of migration as it adapts to the altered environment.

The notion of a sacred space is not of a fixed point in this vast wilderness of sea ice and islands, but rather an unending succession of fleeting sites, briefly invested with the importance of a homeland. The changing environment over the immensity of the northern tundra dictates a certain spatial density among the reindeer. Rarely will they gather in large herds, unlike the caribou of North America, and the lone reindeer that I observe from my window is typical of the spread of their population.

The new climate of the high Arctic has established a temperature regime where snow cover and partial melting may be frequently followed by a refreezing. 'Gololyod' or hungry ice can generate an impenetrable layer of hard ice, which can cause the deaths, through starvation, of many thousands of reindeer.* As I continue to look from the window the reindeer fades and vanishes as mist now rolls in from the fiord to accompany the low cloud.

13.00 hours. The mist and cloud have gradually dispersed as we prepare the boat for a trip to Gritviken and the cliffs for springtail work. The boat passes slowly through the extensive brash ice and growlers that have entered the fiord during the early hours and we check a large block of ice that has an unusual colouring smeared along its flanks. Close inspection shows the staining to be moraine deposit and not the remnants of a bear kill. At Gritviken I leave the others to their research and head south to the outwash of a small glacier that is ablating from the heights of Haavimbfjellet. I pass the old discarded hut and climb along the shore cliffs. From the heights I sit and take the weight of the rifle from my shoulder. Glancing back at the hut, its crumbling structure is dwarfed within the expansive surface of grey tundra.

* Gareth Rees and Fiona Danks. Scott Polar Research Institute.

14.00 hours. I reach the East German hut and commence sketching, but soon the paper is too wet to work as a low drizzle sets in from the surface of the fiord. I decide to record the hut on camera during this initial visit. On close inspection the hut is closed firmly and a rusty lock prevents entry into a dark interior visible through a small porthole window. Through this circular eye I can see a work surface of splintered wood in the foreground. Beyond, a leather upholstered seat extends along the dark panelled wall to a desk and another porthole, which throws a beam of light down upon an open notebook and a couple of pencils. The whole interior, like a ship's cabin, exudes a warmth of old wood, within the discipline of a confined space. I circumnavigate the area of glacial debris and pick up some reindeer antlers. It is a mournful place and the cloud now obscures the views above a height of one hundred feet, and as I make my return to the drop off point I glance back and notice that the hut is placed centrally on the glacial outwash amid the streams of meltwater. A solitary spot now bounded by the steep mountains inland and a necklace of ice, abandoned along the shoreline by the outgoing tide. I descend to the discarded hut and sit awhile within its remaining shelter. Water drips through the roof, but there is still a semblance of comfort in the old interior. It has become familiar to me and I place a small fantail feather on the wooden surface and study it closely. It is delicate and I place it safely in my glasses case for the return to base.

I reach drop off point and while the others finish their day's work I continue northwards along the shore towards the outlines of a weather station. Passing the tide of ice I notice a fall of temperature as I study the accumulated brash. Within the Arctic Sea areas there is a circular movement of ice floe and during the past twenty-four hours this clockwise spin of ice has entered the confined space of Kongsfjord. As I near the weather station the sounds of the ice increase to a high-pitched clicking, like the splintering of glass on light shingle or the sound of knitting needles. The early explorers were often confused and blighted by this floe of ice within the high latitudes and when attempting to reach the pole may have found themselves being carried south, further from 90 degrees north by the day. Like a moving stairway, this drift would be relentlessly erasing their northern path.

18.8.2006. 4.00 hours. Restlessly I look from the window and can see sunlight catching the upper slopes of Zeppelinfjellet. The eccentric tilt of the earth has created the saucer of light in which I now find myself. The improved weather is welcome and visibility within the fiord is much improved on yesterday. I study the map and see that the main glacier entering the fiord to the south has clear signs of a retreat. At the snout of the Kronebreen and Conwaybreen glacier a blue dotted line traces the 1990 position of its greatest extent. At some distance from this the 1998 front is drawn in more definitely and behind this the white mass of the ice is still in place. From the scale of the map it appears that there has been a maximum retreat of half a kilometre in eight years or over sixty metres per annum. I draw on the map the approximate position of the 1936 ice front gathered from the study of old maps. It is far out into the waters of Kongsfjorden.

10.00 hours. We decide to take the boat to Kronebreen at the southern limit of the fiord, where I shall be dropped to work on studies of the fragmenting ice as it calves from the glacier. Nick is concerned about my isolation at this point, but with good weather and a calm sea surface he judges that the risk is not unacceptably high, as long as I do not linger, before heading to Gtitviken to join Roger and the others at the cliffs. Nick Cox, as base commander of the Ny-Alesund research centre, has all the experience of many seasons in the Arctic. Once on the beach I decide on a deepfield study and set to work, while keeping a watchful eye for the threat of bears. Brash ice clicks along the shoreline and thunderous collapses of ice tumble into the water from the main glacier; these sounds of ice are interspersed by a silent state that is beyond the threshold of our customary hearing. The isolation of this remote place is truly deepfield and heightens my sense of vulnerability as cold begins to affect the progress of my drawing and I slow down. I am forced to improvise details of the ice front and concentrate momentarily on the racing sky overhead. Frequently stopping to look around for polar bear, I begin to absorb the circuit of terrain, noting the distances between my kneeling position and the cover of rock debris that sprawls from the steep slopes of Nielsenfjellet.

There is a dreadful, overbearing familiarity to this place and I stop drawing and continue my vigilant scanning of the surrounding surfaces. I quickly note details upon the sheet of paper, weighed down by a rock, and take a series of photographs for later working. The glacier has produced its own microclimate, air temperature is chill and a strong wind begins to descend towards me from the glaciers surface, disturbing my paper. Heeding Nick's warnings I am forced to gather my equipment and head along the fiord shoreline towards Gritviken. Weather continues to deteriorate and the boat is no longer an option, as sea swell has entered the fiord from the north, creating a choppy surface of small breakers. The sandy shoreline soon gives way to a hard surface of glacial debris that slows my progress and I continue into a stiff breeze from the north. After an hour of walking I find a large reindeer antler: the surface of the antler is clean, with a chalky texture and I place it into my rucksack with some difficulty and continue along the shore. Sea birds follow me, including fulmar, arctic skua and the small energetic arctic terns. Before reaching the East German hut I am forced to cross a swift flowing glacial stream. It is full of mud and sand creating a brown wash. Large boulders within the main channel make the crossing more difficult and I am forced to wade into waist-deep waters as I sink into the fine glacial debris of the river bed.

15.30 hours. Arrival at Gritviken and the welcome sounds of the nesting kittiwakes. I sit within the warming sun to dry my clothes and work on a rock study of the cliff face as Roger, Gordana and Yelena complete their work for the day. Nick negotiates the boat to the shore, careful to avoid the increasing sea ice in the turbulent water, and loads the equipment and spare gun before departing for base with Gordana and Yelena. Roger and I will walk back again along the shore, taking time to study the surface of the Midtre Lovenbreen glacier and complete some sketching, while Roger observes the surrounding area.

My unease at the deepfield site continued throughout the day as the presence of the bear permeated my thoughts during the walk back to base. The glacier of Midtre Lovenbreen had displayed all the familiar features of a rapid retreat within the apron of ablation and I was able to record the sounds of meltwater from a number of points. The hazards were not only possible bear attack. Hills of moraine left by the receding ice are unconsolidated, so that collapse exposes a sub-surface world of caverns and slipways, created when large sections of ice broke from the main glacier to become embedded in the clays and shingles. The melt of these ice masses leaves a fragile, honeycombed zone that has been riven and drilled by the departing ice,

As we walked, so my actions were becoming steadily orientated towards the presence of this formidable creature. We wandered along the glacial washes of the shore, binoculars dangling from our necks, pausing every thirty or forty metres to search for bears. Like the Pomori sailors during their long exile, my daily routines were being dictated by the chance of confrontation. The parallel existence of this beast, its upright stance as it consciously hunts its quarry and the long period of hibernation compared to our tiny death of daily sleep placed the bear centrally upon a path that leads towards death. There seemed to exist many connecting strands between us, in a contract of hunter and hunted. Early explorers had died of trichinosis by eating undercooked polar bear meat, causing symptoms similar to scurvy. Those who did not die from this poisoning would suffer from a melancholy brought on by consuming their kill. The bear, like the lion, is not readily consumed and in this it represents the boundary between us and the chaos of the wild place, where the hunted die a death, like a light that dims and fades.

19.8.2006. 19.00 hours. My considerations of the way of the bear have remained. Weather conditions have deteriorated as the inflow of sea ice from the expanses of the Barents Sea gradually alters the surface of the fiord. This migrating ice, mirrored in the clouds above, brings a sea change. Cold air and summer sun combine to produce a sea fog that rolls over the chill waters.

As I make my way over the rough surface track towards the jetty, so a curtain of fog envelops the cluster of buildings that line the waterfront of Ny-Alesund. I approach a large wooden chalet that serves as the bar. Twice a week it opens to the personnel of the base, where the various nationalities can meet and ease through an hour or so of relaxation. Boots are lined up outside the open door as I enter the dark interior. At the bar a group of Norwegian glaciologists are in discussion about the state of ice retreat in recent years. I leave them to their discussion and sit by the window. Beyond the immediate tundra stands the airship tower, just visible in the drifting fog. Ny-Alesund had been the focal point of the world's attention several

times during the decade of the twenties. In 1925 Roald Amundsen attempted to reach the North Pole from Ny-Alesund with the seaplanes N24 and N25. The expedition had been forced into a landing on the ice at 88 degrees north and the explorers had toiled for three weeks to construct a makeshift airstrip in order to return to Ny-Alesund. The following year Amundsen had returned with the American Lincoln Ellesworth and the Italian Umberto Nobile in order to set out over the ice in the airship 'Norge'. Departing on 11 May 1926, they landed at Teller in Alaska two days later, having passed over the pole. The event was given a rather low profile in the press, coinciding as it did with the General Strike, and there was some doubt cast as to how exact the flight of the airship had been in relation to the pole itself.

'At two o'clock this morning, the flight had so far been successful, and it may be presumed that the Norge then crossed the North Pole. Telegrams to the newspapers here show that at midnight the Norge had reached latitude 89 degrees north, longitude 12 degrees east. It was misty and a slight breeze was blowing. The temperature was 10.4 degrees fahrenheit. The airship was travelling at a height of 2,360 feet.'
- Reuter.
The Daily Telegraph. Thursday 13 May 1926.

Ny-Alesund was also the site for the 1928 attempt to the pole by Nobile with the airship 'Italia'. Unfortunately the expedition ended in disaster as the Italia crashed onto the ice to the north of the archipelago, killing half of the crew. Amundsen formed a rescue party in the seaplane 'Latham', but it disappeared and Amundsen and his crew were never seen again. The 'white eagle of Norway', so highly regarded by the Norwegian population, was thought to have survived on some remote, icebound shore.

Looking beyond the tower in the light of late summer, the events of that decade seem all the more eccentric. However, there seems an appropriateness about a first sighting of the pole from the air; a tropospheric arrival above a surface of shifting ice and a landless expanse. It had been a strange conquest, skimming above a white magnetic desert for that alien like glimpse of a zone of time.

20.8.2006. 8.00 hours. During the early hours the low cloud and fog had dispersed and I now look out across the fiord as an energetic sky of cumulus clouds scud across the waters. Sea ice still enters from the north and a line of growlers extends south from the island of Blomstrandhalraga. 15.00 hours. I am dropped onto the beach of Brandelpynten Lykt, lying north from the base, and walk across a broad plain of glacial moraine to Stuphallet. A small field hut provides shelter from the cold winds and I commence work upon a deepfield drawing of Blomstrandbreen where the glacier enters the fiord on the opposite shore. The air is clear, making the glacier appear much nearer. Reindeer graze nearby and occasionally move to a fresh patch of tundra vegetation. From the cliff face behind where I sit, the clinkerous sound of rock fall on scree breaks the silence of this outwash plain. I concentrate upon my drawing and make good progress with the clear details of the collapsing glacial front. Almost continuous sun warms my back and a squadron of barnacle geese pass overhead on a northerly course.

In the hut there is no furniture except for a simple wooden bench and an ornate stove in the corner. The hut is reinforced as protection against polar bear and I sit within the small doorway and glance through the slim visitors' book. Most of the entries are written in Norwegian, but I find a short note from an old colleague who had been with me in Antarctica. Peter Boelen had been drilling soil cores in 2002, at the foot of the bird cliff and as I look out at the cliff I imagine him clambering over the scree. Outside the hut I pick up empty cartridges that have become firmly embedded within the soft mat of tundra moss.

18.00 hours. Returning towards base, I sit awhile by the Bayelva river. It is fed by red muddy waters that stream from the glaciers and have become braided into numerous meandering channels. I rest by the hut that overlooks this torrent of water and ahead of me I can see the glaciers in retreat, each now contained and isolated within their own individual valley. The scene before me fades as cloud builds from

the north. Soon the sun will dip beneath the horizon, marking the crucial end of the northern light. It will be a time when this great scene of melt that spreads before me becomes held within the grip of winter, frozen momentarily into silence.

21.8.2006. 12.00 hours. The Midtre Lovenbreen glacier twists its way down from the heights of Skiferloppen, some five kilometres from the shoreline of Kongsfjorden. Before washing out over the moraine it constricts between two masses of rock; to the north the Sherdahlfjellet and to the south the Stattofjellet, each standing at over fifteen hundred feet. The Midtre Lovenbreen, like all the Spitzbergen glaciers, is in steady retreat and at its snout it is an active area of ablation. In its full extent the glacier would have reached what are now a necklace of small islands within the fiord that include Loven, Midt, Oyane and Juttaholmay, all visible in the midday sun.

I make my way through the hills of moraine as I leave the open expanse of the shoreline. Rising slowly towards the ice, I leave the sounds of meltwater and begin to walk upon the frozen glacier. With little fresh snow my footprints are hardly visible upon the glass-like surface. A large crevasse has formed, parallel to the main thrust of the glacier, and I record the sounds of water, which rise from the blue depths, twisting and turning below me.

17.00 hours. I make my way through the hills of push moraine, as I descend from the glacier, and find easy access to the outwash plain that splays out onto the tundra.

This is a place of comfort, with its broad sweep and wide views that reduce the likelihood of confrontation with a bear. The surface is one of soft moss, bone fragments and the discarded antlers of reindeer. The reindeer have departed for now, possibly to some northern shore. I sit on the soft surface. The waters of the fiord are still, reflecting clear, inverted images from the distant shore. A dull thud of glacial movement comes from Conwaybreen to the south, carrying over the mirrored surface. The air is clear and the 'tricona', a line of pyramidal peaks, are still sharply defined on the far horizon beyond the fiord and its glaciers. I keep still, very still, as the distant sounds of meltwater produce a soussos-like sound in the cool air. Around me the glaciers are all in a slow movement; the gravitational slide of ice had been held, but now the melt undermines these glaciers. Beyond the shores, brash ice and slow-moving growlers collide within the listless drift of water.

Walking upon the broken surface, scattered rib parts and the debris of rock spread before me. This tundra surface, described through the centuries, presents a microscopic world of slow decay.

> 'For in all the North Iland I did not see a cart-load of good earth: yet went I on shoare in the many places and in the Iland of white sand, there is nothing else but mosse and small thornes scattered here and there, withered and dry.'
>
> Jacques Cartier, French mariner, Labrador, 1534.

This most tenuous and refined of land surfaces exists firmly within our notions of the north. It would be the first contact with these lands that would dictate our later interpretations. In this, the effect of an endless expanse of partly frozen tundra interspersed with moss and bog would have thrown the imaginative spirit into an endless spiral. Daunted by that relentless horizon, eyes would avert skywards, gazing into the complexity of atmospheric circulation. For those who look to ground, the intricacy of microscopic detail and traces of animals that exist in this wilderness would commence an intimate and long contact with the animistic world. Where ever the gaze fell, the birth of a northern mythology was set in motion by these simple early footsteps. Those initial impressions of 'north' would have incubated during the long dark winters. Early travellers within the high Arctic would have dwelt in the eccentric seasons, with their long darkness, to be finally broken by endless day. Thus were perpetuated the myths that have been constructed upon this broken surface.

I continue my straight line of walking. Underfoot, the moss provides a spring to my step as I follow a course that is parallel to the shore of the fiord. Occasionally I stop and look back, taking in any irregular features of the surface, but there are few that break the uniformity of the tundra. Within this terrain of glacial retreat I am aware of a great reversal of force, as the departing ice leaves a landscape that is in a state of repose, inert and lacking momentum. The remnants of ice that can now be seen around the fiord present a new condition of the ice that places our glacial orientation into confusion. Gravity seems defied as the ice draws back into the dark shadows of the upper slopes.

19.00 hours. At Ny-Alesund base I look back at the Midtre Lovenbreen glacier; it appears ridiculously close and hardly the distance of two hours' walking that I spent completing the journey. Within the fiord a large growler drifts slowly in the mid distance. Cloud cover is still high and the tricona are visible to the south, though not with the same clarity as earlier.

23.00 hours. I walk down to the jetty. Looking north I see that the cloud cover has broken, and along the polar horizon golden rays now highlight a thin tracery of cloud fragments. At midnight the sun makes contact with the hard line of the sea, thus heralding the beginning of the dark night of winter. This first chill touch brings a small and imperceptible shading of the light. That eccentric geometry of spheres contrived this moment and makes special this brief waterside walk, amid the call of tern and the graceful glide of a fulmar. Out across the fiord, large blocks of ice drift south within the new day.

22.8.2006. 10.00 hours. The smooth waters of the fiord are interspersed with a medley of floating ice. With little wind the boat makes good time to Gritviken, where I set to work recording the grounded brash ice that has been abandoned by the gradual ebb of an outgoing tide. Roger, Gordana and Yelena are already at work on springtail collection, high above the shore with its spread of abandoned rucksacks and equipment. The chaotic flight of terns fill the air, as the sounds of ice become lost amid the frenzied cries of the gulls. I head south along the water's edge, taking a circuitous route around the glacial deposit that has protruded into the fiord from the lower mountain slopes. I pass the discarded hut and climb beyond a low cliff to a broad tundra surface and the East German hut sitting in isolation some fifty metres from the shores of the fiord. The hut was constructed when East Germany had formed an independent science group during the nineteen seventies; from its weathered surfaces the hut looks much older, belonging to an earlier age of polar science. Having acquired the key from base I unlock the heavy door and enter the darkness of the interior, with its soft comfort of wooden surfaces. The two porthole windows give views in different directions, providing a clear panorama of the surrounding terrain. The deep sound of ice collapse from Conwaybreen carries across the water as I sit and sketch first the outer details of the hut construction and then the interior.

My familiarity with this hut has formed from a number of visits made in various weather conditions. The windless air of earlier has now been replaced by a keen breeze from the north. Cloud levels have fallen and I can see the approach of a bank of rain. A large cushion of air now descends as distant peaks and mountain slopes are erased from view and the cloud continues its descent to the cold water surface.

I read the entries in the visitors' book. It is an old exercise book of lined paper and on its worn surface I read the different translations of hut book, Hytte bok and hutten buch, beneath the scrawled date of August 1980. With a break in the rain and sleet I return to the shoreline to record a final part of the ice tape for the day. My

recording is interrupted by the crackle of the radio as Nick checks on our field positions. From the conversations I learn that Roger and the others will be making their way to the East German hut from the Gritviken site.

Realising that my solitude will soon be over, I re-enter the sanctity of the hut, the tysker hytta, and read more entries from the book. They tell of polar bear sightings and encounters. From the open notebook I look out from the interior into a world of half light. The porthole window is coated in a thick dust, but I can make out the grey decay of the tundra surface; bears have trodden upon these expectant surfaces. Within the hut contents exist singularly, each with its specific sense of place. All seem somehow to be essential. A family photograph is pinned to a wooden boarding, fading in the constant light of a polar summer; bleached and blinded, the photographed figures look out on polar scenes, never to be seen or imagined.

14.15 hours. The cloud has now consumed the mountains across the fiord; water and scattered ice now give an impression of fading into infinity as I sit and write in the last moments of solitude. Looking north I can just make out the three small figures as they traverse the moraine. Visibility is still falling and rainfall now becomes more prolonged. Moments are now used within the hut to absorb small details; the grain of old wood, the rusting hinges and old lamp fittings amid the ordered functionalism of the shelves and work surfaces. The sense of time passing is palpable, amid the solitary moments of heightened emotion.

Finally, the sound of footsteps upon the clinkerous moraines and the breaking of silence, as that world onto which I have been gazing gently fades.

23.8.2006. Beyond the small bay of Kolhamna, to the north of Ny-Alesund, a thin line of beach extends into the fiord. This spit of land forms part of Brandalpynton and from the map it can be seen that an arcuate foreland has spread into the waters of Kongsfjorden. Fine sediment has been sifted from the glacial moraines and carried to this point, where waters entering the fiord meet those of the outgoing and refracted forces, causing the waves to drop their material. It is a subdued, low-lying beach that contrasts with the heavy glacial moraine and gravels of the other beaches. Situated away from steep mountain slopes and the descent of glaciers, it is a place of open terrain and active sky. Brandalpynton points to the north and the open polar sea. At this latitude, the tenuous strand rests, like some final shore of the earth.

11.00 hours. Sitting within the hut at Brandelpynton, rain and sleet sound on the tin roof. Picking up the binoculars from the table by the window I look towards Ossian Sarsfjellet, rising in the distance at the southern end of the fiord. At the base of the massif the shoreline is shrouded in ice, where the glacier is in the process of calving into the waters. It is a pluvial outlook. The shore in front of the hut is strewn with driftwood. A fulmar flies low across the grey water and passes directly over the hut. Terns hover and dive along the shoreline, breaking the smooth surface. With the passing of the rain I decide to walk to the point, searching among the piles of driftwood as I make my way along the upper tidal margin. At Brandelpynton point I stand by an old weather recording structure, which is now in a state of collapse. From the excited calls of the terns I am probably close to their nesting areas. I look towards the gates of the north, in the form of two distinct headlands partly lost within the passing rain. Between them the grey wall of weather and the agitated sea surface are indistinguishable.

13.00 hours. From Brandelpynton point I take a circular route across the broad plain of tundra. In parts the surface is composed of a thick moss, cushioning my steps. Occasionally I pass the stone circles that have been produced by a frost heave, as the cold winters of earlier years froze the ground water, causing the surface to swell and dislodge the shattered fragments upon this exposed surface. My wandering brings me to the expanse of the glaciers Vestre and Austre Broggenbreen. Both valley glaciers are clearly in retreat, and have filled a vast lowland area with the accumulation of outwash gravels. Melt channels meander haphazardly, twisting and turning before entering the muddy torrent that rages pass me, on its course to the open waters of the fiord.

Evidence of climate change is widespread across Scandinavia. Finland had lost over half of its permafrost by 1975, and elsewhere in these northern lands methane emission can be seen on both land surface and sea bed. Much of south-east Svalbard is covered in pockmarks, indicating a rapid release of this potent greenhouse gas. It is a process that continues around the entire belt of the high latitudes.

Nils Wladimir hut rests upon a slender terrace, overlooking this scene of ablation. I prepare a coffee from the supplies within the small functional kitchen and sit outside in the sun of early afternoon. All about me the landscape is in its slow geological state of change. Before me the retracting ice and snow appear to return to the upper slopes, ingested into the fabric of rock, leaving a broken and scratched imprint of the 'great weight'. A torn and ravaged skin, reduced, puddled and bled, lying beneath the skies of today. Looking back to the expansive waters of the fiord, the Brandelpynton spit fingers its way to the north, gaining its fine load at each turn of wave. And the north's expectant void, filled with its tracery of time lines and its thin magnetic air, will see the retreat of ice. The great sink of these high latitudes,

pulling that old white wreck to the planet's inner core, leaving nothing but an ocean swell and a clear horizon.

20.30 hours. I sit within the Mellagret bar. Through the open door I can see Amundsen's tower. It has a solitary red light at its top. There is a slight fading of the light and the land has a dark melancholy held within the rock. The eye of summer is closing and the long darkness is approaching. A wall of sleet carries across the level surface of tundra, partly erasing the tower and diluting the small red light into a flickering blur of crimson as a frozen rain drums on the window.

Part Four
Whale Spirits and Trampolines

Alaska

Sketch the Seventh.

Across the bay, within the vast eye of a frozen
world, the shallop is lowered onto the floe.
Two objects in white space,
the vessels diverge and the dark form of the
shallop is gradually distanced from the
mother ship.

Three figures sit huddled together as one
places a blanket around the shoulders of
his young son.

This northern light, amid the endless
train of frozen rivers, will hold
their deaths, a silent image upon
smooth glass.

> From the mutiny in the ice of James Bay 1609/10
> in which Henry Hudson and his son were left to starve
> and freeze.

Sketch the Eighth.

'They first pointed to the ships, eagerly asking, what great creatures those were. Do they come from the sun or moon? Do they give us light by night or by day? Sacheuse told them that he was a man, that he had a father and mother like themselves; and pointing to the south, said that he came from a distant country in that direction. To this they answered, 'That cannot be, there is nothing but ice there.'

John Ross. An account of the discovery of the Polar Eskimo.1819.

Whale Spirits and Trampolines.

Barrow Arctic Science Consortium.2007.
Northern Alaska.
Elevation. Sea Level.
Latitude. 72 degrees north.

Journey to Anchorage. 5.7.2007.
From 35000' we pass over Greenland's southern shores. Numerous flickering images can be seen down the length of the aircraft, highlighting the white triangular land mass. The small outline of the plane moves slowly, inexorably across the screens, westwards over the Davis Strait and arcing down to Goose Bay and the Canadian northlands. The daylight zone can be seen flooding across most of the North American land mass, while further west the Pacific Ocean lies beneath the shadow of night. To the north the lands of Alaska, Baffin and Greenland are resplendent in the perpetual light of summer.

The great rollercoaster of flight follows the broad wave that divides the day from night, as we drop to the southern lands of Texas and from Houston we rise again in flight to Anchorage and the north. Held within that zone of light, energetic clouds appear to explode upwards, pulsing into the higher belts of the atmosphere. Heading north we pass over the geometry of irrigation of Arizona, Nevada and Utah, before rising over the western seaboard and the Rockies to crest the glaciated peaks of Alaska.

The great wave of the nights shadow engulfs us as we approach the city of Anchorage, while the northern shores of Alaska remain firmly within daylight.

5.7.2007. 23.00 hours. 119 West 12th Street, Anchorage.
Sitting in front of a wide window I look out towards the mountains. The quietness of the north lies heavily upon the land, held in the light of late evening. Beyond the lights and highways of Anchorage true wilderness extends to the eastern horizon, lying within its long twilight. In Alaska they talk of the 'lower 48', referring to the rest of the USA, as if to emphasise their northern location within the expanse of high latitudes: while in the 'lower 48' they look to Alaska as a land that trails as much to the west as to the north. It is a strange dysfunctional relationship and I suspect it underlies the American unease with the whole idea of' north. In the Eurasian mind there is acceptance of land masses trailing north-wards beyond the Arctic Circle and onto the broad hinterland of the tundra.

Alaskans are proud of their state, with its distance from their southern counterparts. Looking across the outskirts of Anchorage I can see the space and scale of its growth. Buildings are low and generous, many recently built as part of the ongoing reconstruction following the devastating earthquake of 1964. The people of Anchorage must have thought that the world had come to an end. The Good Friday earthquake struck at 5.36 pm on 27 March, and with a Richter magnitude of 9.2, it is still the most powerful recorded quake in North American history. Within four minutes much of the city had been destroyed and some parts of Alaska were liquefied by immense pressure. Landslides and tsunamis pulverised wide areas, as vertical displacement of the land surface reached up to thirty-eight feet. Ocean floor movement sent devastating waves against the north-west coast of North America, while the land areas to the northern tundra were shaken like a basket of broken crockery. The town of Portage subsided below high water level and was abandoned entirely, and for many communities the relationship between land and sea level had changed forever. Classified as a megathrust earthquake along a subduction zone, it was sufficient to vibrate the earth, as water sloshed about in the wells of South Africa.

Looking out into the half light, with its web of telegraph poles and wires strung between the wooden buildings, the city seems to be slowing down towards the hour of midnight.

6.7.2007. 11.00 hours.
With its observation decks and telescopes, the Begich-Boggs visitor centre was constructed to provide views of the Portage Glacier. However, the glacial retreat has been so fast that it can no longer be seen from the centre. Since the 1900s the glacier has lost over five miles of ice. Situated almost fifty miles to the north of Anchorage, the rapid reduction of the Portage ice is a scale of change that can be seen across the entire northlands of Canada and the United States. The deep irony of the retreat is reinforced by a presentation for the tourists, called the 'voices from the ice', during which they gaze out onto the expansive waters of the lake while listening to this whisper from the past. As I make my way out of the centre I notice the flight of a sea plane as it follows the contours of the distant mountain slopes, like a moth tracing along a strip of light. The high pitch of the engines carries over the waters.

16.00 hours.
I trek east towards the smaller valley of the Byron Glacier and follow the sounds of cascading meltwaters until I leave the path, with its tourist notices and bear warnings and climb over the broad area of moraine. Large boulders have been left by the glacier in a train of deposition, indicating a temporary halt in the process of ablation.

Beyond the debris of moraine I begin to walk upon the apron of old ice. It is brittle and breaks beneath my step, slowing my progress towards the upper combes of the glacier. The surface is riddled with the effect of ice worm and discoloured by the dirt of pollution, which gives an appearance of thin ash. As I slowly ascend the foothills, I sense a transition into an element of wilderness, far removed from the orderly world of the lower lake shore and the visitor centre. Large areas of North America have been preserved in the compromising hold of the national parks, but here, elevated away from the highways and the voices of the ice, I glimpse that truth of a wilderness that can only be seen in the solitude of high places.

High altitude and high latitude combine to produce this theatre of the wild and as I make for the steep incline of the glacier surface ahead of me, so the first hazardous crevasses come into view.

I sit awhile upon the hard ice and look down towards Lake Portage. The silence is broken by the sound of engines somewhere below me and I eventually spot the small plane as it heads towards the lake. The high pitch fills the valley in which I sit, obscuring all the sounds of melt until the plane slows and lands upon the lake, sending out symmetrical waves across the blue-grey waters.

9.7.2007. 7.00 hours.
The rail journey from Anchorage to Fairbanks is boasted as the finest railway trip in the world. I sit within the station waiting room amid the bustle of preparation for departure. Beyond the wide windows I can see a steady fall of rain beneath a solid layer of low cloud. A single track of line stretches away to the north and the expansive sidings are littered with the debris of old trucks and freight rolling stock. A sense of impending departure is tangible, as groups stand nervously, gazing out onto the wet scene beyond the station. I sit opposite a brightly lit sidetrack espresso, pondering whether to take a relatively cheap coffee hit while it is at a convenient

distance, when a group of men make straight for the sidetrack, all peaked caps and chequered shirts. My attention is diverted by the loudspeaker, as a polite though high pitched voice announces that the next train to arrive will be for Fairbanks. As the information continues to cascade from the old speaker system, people shift their feet and edge towards the gate, as the large outline of a blue and yellow locomotive cuts out the grey light of the window.

I let the main block of passengers force their way through the narrow gate, and take in more details of the departure hall: a line of drawings ends abruptly with a large moose head that has been nailed to the wall. A distance chart shows Fairbanks at an impressive three hundred and fifty-six miles and another notice states that here at Anchorage, we are at thirty-eight feet elevation. My observations are halted by another shrill announcement, throwing out the question, 'Are we all ready to board?' which is immediately answered by a chorus of 'Yes!'

I ponder this being applied to commuters at East Croydon on a wet Monday morning at 7.45. We board and I immediately notice from the seats that we are all going to travel backwards for the entire journey, or I have been mistaken in my calculations of where north and south are orientated. I am reassured as the train performs a small circular manoeuvre before its departure. The rain continues and I recline my seat to a loud sigh from behind me and contemplate the journey ahead. The voice from the departure lounge has suddenly returned, filling the slow-moving train and informing us, in muffled tones, of eating times before explaining that the speaker is not loud enough. The microphone is thrown down in disgust. Minutes later a young hostess works her way along the entire length of the train, apologising for the lack of sound and giving a potted history of Anchorage, pausing at every two or three tables. From where I sit I can hear this repeated monologue as it fades into the next carriage, each account getting briefer and more clipped. Finally, a jumbled, inaccurate drawl compacted into three sentences is followed by the challenge, 'are there any questions?' No one dares to utter.

The final performance in our departure comes in the form of another hostess, making her way down the carriage and asking each passenger where they are from and what do they do. To each answer she gives an 'oh wow.' At this point I stare fixedly out of the window to be confronted with the Anchorage gravel pits and an unending blur of trees.

9.50 hours. Wassali, and the first stop on this northern journey, which is already producing a dulling sensation as I continue to look from the window at the falling rain and the discarded rolling stock, the bland architecture and the brutal truth that something rather crucial has been left behind. A dawning sense of regret sinks in as the 'Dead End' signs begin to appear along the track. I am within that apron of land that seems to skirt all the northern polar areas, where man has managed to degrade the environment with an ugly and inconsiderate footprint. The train slows and we pass Dead Dog Saloon.

North of Anchorage the landscape is dominated by the immense system of the Susistna river, fed by the glaciers of the north within the Denali National Park. Glacial rock flour, mud and marsh support thin tree growth to produce a badlands, while to the east rise the mountains of Talkeetna.

Wassali and a long line of identical settlements seem to be inhabited by the 'didn't quite' people. They didn't quite make it to the splendour of true north, and they didn't quite have enough money to get back to the south. They remain adrift in this land hell, in the form of forest, with its infinity of shrinking trees from which one may at some time emerge into the polar light, upon the soft tundra step of a northern land. 11.50 hours. As we pull into Talkeetna Station I look out of the window to see the Sixty-two Degree Latitude Lodge.

17.00 hours. I move from the carriage and sit within the panoramic section of the train, in the form of a glass bubble elevated above the normal seating and giving the sensation of being within a bullet as it fires north.

I read from the free brochure that the City of Fairbanks was founded when a Captain Barnette grounded his ship in the shallow water of the Chena river and could go no further. A place founded by someone who could not get away does not bode well for Fairbanks. It appears that the 'didn't quite' people come from a long line.

The train rolls on slowly, passing the surfaces of Denali Park. As we head north under a clear sky I notice a change in the tree height. Thin birch and spruce are scattered across the widening horizon. Apparently, the old telegraph company didn't quite make it either, and discarded poles in various states of collapse run along, parallel to the track. The landscape is now more spacious as trees thin and small glacial ponds give an impression of some primordial state. In most histories the people run out of land, but here the land defeated the people and continued on its march to a distant horizon.

Fairbanks lies close to the Arctic Circle and claims to be a gateway to the frozen polar world. Just twenty miles to the north the small township of North Pole gives the necessary ambience to the claim. As the train nears Fairbanks the engine whistle announces our arrival; a mournful sound, cushioned by the falling rain on the Chena flatlands.

10.7.2007. 7.30 hours.
Sixty-two degrees fahrenheit had flashed upon the street board last night and now, as I sit within the diner, it feels warmer still. After a night struggling against the sound of a generator from an adjacent building site, I delicately ease into the downstairs breakfast area and take a seat by a fan and enjoy the circulation of air.

Conversation rolls around a group of middle-aged locals. They talk of incursions from wild animals, including a fox in the yard and a bear up at the North Pole township, along with tax issues and the location of wood piles along the highway. All of these comments are delivered in a state of high jollity, as an imposing figure by the name of Nelson, joins the group. Nelson sits down clumsily and joins in the debate on the collective pronoun for ducks.

The talk concentrates on the local bird sightings; a raptor was seen by the lake; possibly a hawk or a falcon. As I continue to eavesdrop, so I realise that the talk is all about the ability of factual recall. It is an exercise in the observations that define their area or their near neighbourhoods, and it becomes interspersed with detailed extracts from the local Fairbanks Daily, that is being passed around the group. 10.30 hours. I consider the world beyond the diner. The bus station over the road and the fleet of four by fours that stream past the window as I finish my coffee, all set the pace for movement. The northern towns have a utility around them which is all about being ready to move on, whether it be the spaces of the north or to the nearby mountains.

The broad screen in the station flashes at seventy-two degrees as I board the bus for the university campus and the museum of the north. The journey takes us out onto the freeway and I am immediately aware of the extent of Fairbanks' sprawling community. The great circular swathe of the freeway passes the churches of god, pioneering centres and megastores, all held in one continuous line of dysfunction. Eventually the bus swings into Alumni Drive and the campus of the University of Alaska. I am intrigued by the prospect of encountering a museum dedicated to a compass point as I leave the bus and make my way through the campus, following the blue arrows to the 'north'. On entry into the museum I am confronted by a poster proclaiming 'the future of ice', and in an instant I am propelled away from the world of the Fairbanks township. I decide on viewing a show of one of the more physical manifestations of the north and book a seat for the aurora show.

As I sit, glazed by the images that flicker on the screen, I gather from the dialogue that the sun produces a state of perpetual storm from which particles jet out into the solar system, carried by powerful winds that take two days to reach earth's atmosphere. At this point some of the audience begin to fidget at the complexity of the technical details, but I hold in and become engrossed in the continuing lecture. The solar particles meet electrons coming out from the earth and collide around the oxygen atoms approximately sixty to seventy miles above the earth's surface. At this point the disillusioned start checking watches to see how much more they have to listen to, with the exception of a spectacled youth sitting at the front. The speaker saves the day by referring to the apparent sounds of the aurora as a mystery. Are they low frequency radio waves, or are they sounds that only some people can hear?

I emerge from the lecture hall with a mixture of bemusement and quiet satisfaction, content that I still have sufficient ignorance to still dream of my first aurora.

Before leaving the museum I wander into the gallery of Alaska and among the displays of old hunting tools and whaling equipment I come to a large glass case containing 'Blue Babe'. Bison Priscus was recently excavated from the ice of the steppe, having roamed across the interior of Alaska during the Wisconsin Period of between 10,000-100,000 years ago. She died about 36,000 years ago, probably killed by a lion. The blue comes from phosphorous in the animal tissue that reacts with

iron in the soil to produce a mineral coating of vivianite. Once this is exposed to the air it becomes brilliant blue. There she hunches, felled by a predator, as if it were yesterday.

12.7.2007. 8.00 hours.
Heavy rain and the prospect of more to follow. As I sit within the diner a deep dislike of rain, forests and flat landscape begins to form and all three lie beyond the window. At this latitude Fairbanks has only six minutes of darkness per day: I consider the prospect of twenty-three hours and fifty-four minutes of daylight rainfall. It is the day of travel to Barrow and the far north and I have until two in the afternoon to fill time.

As I receive my coffee I am acknowledged with a nod and a wave from the same group of locals as yesterday. I allow their conversation to float over me as I peruse the magazines, occasionally picking up the thread of what they are saying. It seems soapy, like the countless American television channels. The world beyond Fairbanks seems a long way off.

15.00 hours. At Fairbanks airport I gaze out at the runways as numerous small planes manoeuvre around the open areas. Seaplanes appear like old bi-planes from an earlier time and the 737 waiting to be fuelled looks like a grounded giant. The leaden skies of earlier have lifted and I look north and imagine a treeless world held within the magnetic light of high latitude.

Rising above Fairbanks I look back at the channels of glacial mud that cut through the greenery of tree cover. At a greater altitude the world of glacial erosion, in the form of pockmarks, lake hollows and moraines, spreads out across the land and we soon pass over the broad snaking mud of the Yukon river.

The 'in-flight' information confirms that Barrow is an unseasonably warm forty-seven degrees and as I consider this and the clear skies ahead, we are brought the flight snack of cougar mountain cookie and Matanuska thunder chips, lightly salted.

After an hour of flight the land surface changes as we rise over the Brookes Range, before descending the North Slope to the ocean margin. We fly over a treeless expanse of tundra, broken by the abandoned courses of rivers that have made their way north from the mountains. A surface of shallow pools and lakes left by river and ice sheet to reveal the glistening blue-black waters.

As we approach the expanse of the Beaufort and Chuckti seas, this broken pane of water gives way to an immense beach surface, left by the outgoing tide of the Pleistocene ice. Remnants of sea ice strung along the coast like white beads signal the direction of drift, as the broken ice collects within the shallow inlets that occasionally disturb the line of this final shore.

Barrow and the scattered communities exist on that littoral zone where the land runs out and where the balance of land and sea levels hang on a worn thread.

Barrow forms the largest of the Arctic North Slope communities. From the air it can be seen to spread along the ruler-straight coast, forming the only break in an otherwise seamless transition from land to sea. Once on the ground having negotiated the airport luggage handling, which mysteriously takes forty-five minutes to unload a pile of well travelled rucksacks, I emerge into a place of sheds and huts, as well as the more substantial inupiat homesteads. The indigenous inupiat families form the great majority of Barrow's population. They have been here for a long time, probably originating across the great land bridge that linked Alaska to Asia. More recently the combined effects of world war and oil discovery of the twentieth century have altered this remote state. Beyond the boundaries of the old town, with its new civic centre and police station, the more functional science bases trail along the coast towards Point Barrow and the most northerly beach of the American mainland.

19.00 hours. Eventually the logistics group of the science base locate a room for me within the lengthy corridors that dominate the building. Within twenty minutes I am on the north shore, standing within the evening sunlight. The sun is still high in the sky and a somewhat dislocated sensation fills my first walk. Sea ice is too far out to glimpse, even with binoculars. Recent seasons have seen a greater break of the link between land and sea ice and subsequently the wildlife has altered its pattern of movement in the endless search for food. The beach forms a low-lying strand composed of glacial shingle that falls away underfoot. The sea is calm and debris of wood and bone flotsam stretches as far as the eye can see. A school of beluga whales are making their way westwards from Point Barrow, breaking the surface with their marble white flanks. As I re-track along the shingle keeping them in view, I see the remains of whale bone, old and yellow, marooned high above the present tidal range.

22.00 hours. Once back at base I can view the sea from my window. A small section of ocean fills the gap between the utility buildings; a tantalisingly active area of polar sea, held within the summer light as one day edges into another.

This remote outpost of scientific research seems held in the very changes that it is monitoring. With the rising sea of ice free water to the north and the lungs of the tundra exhaling methane to the south, the Barrow Arctic Science Consortium stands as an island of reasoning amid the chaos of a changing world.

13.7.2007. 6.00 hours.
I wake to a thick mist. However, the flag of the stars and stripes is fluttering above the adjacent building, indicating that a brisk wind from the south will soon carry it over the ocean. I make my way to the breakfast room and by 8.00 hours the mist has gone. Over the radio news of the plight of the polar bear states that female bears are now having to den on land rather than on the hazardous sea ice, which has become unreliable.

The walls of the corridors are covered with the findings of the various science groups, including graphs of local permafrost thawing and destabilisation close to Point Barrow and the air-sea carbon dioxide flux over Copper Island. The bulletins are concerned with local and regional changes, but the implications are global.

Looking across the top of the world plays upon our perceptions of a credible map. As I walk in a westerly direction along the shingle beach I am aware that this line of latitude touches the land mass of northern Asia. That across the narrow Bering

Strait Siberia extends west in a seemingly endless tundra, until the line of latitude clips northern Scandinavia and bisects the Greenland ice cap before entering the chaotic geography of the Canadian northland. When Vitus Bering departed from Kamchatka in 1741 and headed east along the volcanic remnants that form the Aleutian Islands, he was establishing a new geography, with a brief and tenuous encounter with the American continent. Accompanying Bering on this two-year voyage was the naturalist G.W. Steller. At the end of a ten-year period of preparation Steller would be granted ten hours to document the natural history of Kayak Island, lying as it does close to the American coast, before being forced to make the return journey.

I have often thought of that task confronting the hapless Steller, as he walked onto those shores. To pit his intellect against the physical challenge of accumulating so much in so little time, overcoming the enormity of an occasion, held like a crystal in the palm of his hand. The whole day would have been weighted in significance as he and his assistant, Lepekhin, set off along the beach. The sands gouged by the trails of the hair seals and the kelp populated by ravens, as they fed on the insects. As the day was slipping from him, Steller would spread all the specimens collected upon the sand so that he could select and enter details in his notebook.

The scientific paper was the first ever written on the natural history of Alaska and would have been patiently catalogued on ship as the expedition made its long homeward journey to Kamchatka. Despite shipwreck at the western extremity of the Aleutian Islands, Steller was able to salvage most of his work for publication.

12.00 hours. From the shore I look to the northern horizon through my binoculars but can see no ice. Visibility is sharp and clear, as seabird flight hovers close to the shore.

The beach material of shingle is occasionally mixed with fine silts and I come across the carcass of a snowy owl, spread upon the smooth surface. The chaotic last moments of life have damaged many of the large feathers, but the broad head is still intact and unblemished. The preoccupations of this northern shore are dominated by the always vigilant watch of the ocean surface. Over the centuries survival on the coast would have relied upon whale and seal. Only occasionally, when caribou are in migration over the tundra, would eyes be turned to the south.

13.00 hours. I join Brian, Laura and Marina from the science consortium and head inland onto the tundra. The vast, swampy surface of moss and grasses is springy underfoot and extends over three hundred miles to the foothills of the Brookes Range.

As we walk over the flat terrain so we disturb dunlins, sandpiper and jaeger, as well as numerous lemmings, which scamper around in the tufted grass. Brian has two boisterous mongrels, one of which is endearingly named Rear Admiral John Franklin. It occurs to me that if the dogs run off into the infinity of the tundra, we

have the prospect of informing the Barrow police force that John Franklin is missing. After an hour of walking in an apparently straight line, there is little variation in the tundra surface other than the gentle swells and undulations that alter the line of the horizon. Small, shallow lakes of dark water begin to hamper our path. Distance is almost impossible to gauge and I glance back at the only landmark in the form of a parked truck, which is now a small, insignificant speck within the tundra desert. The sense of sky as a vast dome is immense, as winds pick up and carry feather and cotton weed and disturb the lake waters.

The experience of the tundra has the effect of concentrating attention on the minutiae of the surface itself, whether on the shoreline or the moss and debris of the

plains. In a land of few definable points I have become aware of a nonscape where, regardless of compass point, the view is unchanging. Thoughts slide towards an infinity of flat horizons. It is difficult to hold onto a landscape which is continually illusive, where the line between hard surface and imagination is uncertain. Within the galleries of the Anchorage Museum I had come across a set of old photographs depicting life in the north. One of the prints had indicated how the inupiat people would occasionally overcome this flat landscape. A ring of faces look up at a child suspended in the air above a sealskin trampoline. Momentarily the elevated child would experience an extended land surface, a new world, stretching out beyond the village. That brief glimpse may contain the sight of a polar bear, the spout of foul liquid from a bowhead whale or possibly a large migration of caribou; food enough for a long dark winter. It is easy to see how the inuit view of the world grew over the span of the centuries. The world spreading out to a form of cold infinity, from the core of their village and lands. And then those strange, unsettling encounters with the European explorers coming, as they did, from some other planet.

20.00 hours. Back on the shoreline my considerations of this tundra microcosm continue as I look out to the altering tones of sky and sea. With a growing awareness I watch the sea surface as a change in the atmospheric conditions unfolds. Mist appears from the west and rolls steadily to the shore; the sea surface changes to gun metal and then into a sequence of zinc tones as light penetrates from the heart of the mist. A small cell of weather passes as I follow its progress eastwards to Point Barrow.

23.00 hours. I sit within my room with the map showing the top of the world spread across the bed. Almost diametric to Barrow lies the Svalbard Archipelago, traced on a line that passes through the North Pole. Between Barrow and the pole the ocean floor encounters a number of obstacles in the form of the Canadian Basin, Fletcher's Ridge and finally the Lomonosov Ridge. For the ocean surface, however, there is no obstacle at all. Clear blue water and white breakers can be seen from my window, continuing on over the north's arcing surface to the pole itself.

17.7.2007. 8.45 hours.   .
The shingle beach extends eastwards to the point. The low profile of the spit traces a pencil thin line between sea and sky as it curves gently to the south, partly enclosing a lagoon.

The day is grey as we prepare for departure on a fleet of quad bikes. A group of students and a team of archaeologists, accompanied by two local bear guides with guns strapped to their vehicles, are revving impatiently on the powerful machines. The destination is Point Barrow, for an archaeological dig to uncover and retrieve ancient inupiat graves. Wave erosion and gravel collapse are causing the old graves to slip into sea along the northern edge of the spit.

With a wave from one of the guides the convoy of noisy quads begins the journey along the shingle, sending a cloud of dust into the sea breeze. Keeping to the upper beach the quads follow the tracks of the previous day and make good progress for the six-mile journey.

Three sites are to be worked today, and as the group begin to prepare for work I decide to go with Perry, one of the guides, for a ride to the distant point of Plover. Three long winters were spent here in the 1850s by the crew of the Plover, dispatched to this remote point in the search for Franklin.

Perry is thin and wiry, of an age that is difficult to assess. We head along the narrow line of the spit for five miles, with the lagoon on our right and the Beaufort Sea to our left. As we speed along the shingle Perry gives a commentary on the debris and the whale bones that litter the shore, and for much of the journey he talks of hunting. We stop by a large skull of a bowhead whale. Perry describes the kill of a seal or bear with various sound effects, not only the gunshot but also the falling creature. Excited by the prospect of whaling, he gives out the sound of whale communication, as well as notable bird calls such as the eider duck. This melody of noise comes from the past, as the shamans of these lands would give such animated performances in their role as storytellers.

For Perry the dominant thought is for the return of the sea ice. It is then that he will look out to sea, and on the horizon will be a thin white band. At present, the wind is from the north and this is a good omen for the awaited return. The whaling fleet of Barrow numbers about forty boats, and the prime catch includes the bowhead, minke and grey whale, as well as the bearded seal. In recent times the whale catch for the Barrow inupiat has been set at forty bowhead. Perry explains that this is quite sufficient for the wider community of the northern coast, including

Wainwright: it has always been sufficient and they have never over-fished. If the bowhead do not show, then they will hunt the seal or even the caribou, with a long chase over the tundra flatlands. At the furthest reach of the spit we stop and dismount. I leave Perry as he reclines on the machine and enjoys a cigarette, and start my customary search along this most remote of beaches. Fine flotsam lines the upper berm of the shallow beach, with small bone parts, bleached wood and shell fragments. Every aspect of this shoreline is small in scale; the slight tidal movement and the gentle action of the wave ripples have refined the beach to a delicate state, where the processes of the sea have almost expired.

With my small bag of found objects I return to Perry and we talk of hunting and the changes of sea ice in recent seasons. He is ambivalent to aspects of such changes and begins to tell me about his digital camera when he notices me struggling to retrieve my pentax from the rucksack. He is full of the technical details and capabilities of the modern camera and is clearly bemused by my old equipment. As we make our way back along the shore, we sight a minke whale as the large head rises slowly out of the water taking in food. We stand still and watch the whale resurfacing, as it tracks slowly to the east and enters an area of shallow water before veering out to sea and the open waters. Perry's disappointment in the whale's freedom is obvious. Had the whale become grounded, he would have started preparations for the kill.

15.00 hours. After completing some preliminary sketches of the exposed graves, I break from the group and walk along the lagoon shoreline and onto the expanse of tundra. The surface is grey with the breakdown of bone fragments and as I scan the horizon of the distant spit, a white covering of bone and dead wood extends on the shingle to Plover Point. The tundra surface of light vegetative growth and bone parts is occasionally broken by the mounds of frost heave. To landward, caribou carcasses become more evident in this vast arena of wild carnage. The traffic of remains lie here in this northern silence like some final resting place, removed from all forces of movement except gravity.

I come to a dried pond where the silt has cracked in the dry winds. In the centre caribou skull and antlers emerge from the copper coloration of deposited mud.

I rejoin the excavations and sit with Perry by one of the graves that is now being exposed. He describes the remains that are now drying out in the afternoon breeze as a 'long time ago whaler' before continuing on the subject of hunting, which is never far from his mind. Apparently the young calf whale produces a particularly tender food, which is normally given to the elders of the community. The hunters will part the mother from the young, so that they can kill the calf in the same way that the orca hunt their food. The whalers do not kill orca, as it is believed that the killer whale will come back to get those who hunted it.

During my conversations with Perry we would frequently cross that tracery divide between what is real and the world of spirit and belief. Like words across time, floating above the level surface of the ice and moving effortlessly from one world to another.

17.00 hours. At the Nuvuk site the day's work is coming to an end, and preparations for the return journey are under way. I train my binoculars to the eastern horizon and glimpse a fragmented line of ice piercing the blue haze of distance. This will be a welcome sight for the whalers, with its prospect of bearded seal and whale. Soon the boats will be making their way across the northern waters, and as I write these notes Perry makes his way to the eastern shore to catch a quick glimpse of the horizon before turning and making a rapid return. The arrival of the sea ice dictates the lives of the inupiat. With no sea ice, what is there to turn the year? Perry's excitement is clear and as we load the quads with equipment his animated conversation can be heard above the group.

18.7.2007. 15.00 hours.

These conversations with Perry and the effect of days at this northern outpost have begun to change my notion of landscape, along with the understanding of the normal relationship between land and sea areas. With the prospect of completely flat surfaces in all compass points, a three hundred and sixty degree panorama offers no variation. The tundra assumes the properties of an ocean and like the view to the north, it exists within a two-dimensional realm.

The significance of the trampoline grows with each passing day, with its brief glimpse of the open page of the land surface. It is with this in mind that I am driven out to the methane monitoring team as they work far out within the tundra sea. The consortium driver by the name of Scott slugs back Coca Cola and wrestles with a radio handset as he drives me along the straight road to the drop off point. In the distance I can see small figures on the horizon.

The geo-chemical area covers a thousand-acre square of the tundra and forms part of the bio-complexity experiment. The methane team is led by Joe von Fischer. Essentially the work is assessing the extent and land surface distribution of methane and carbon dioxide emissions. As I arrive at the site Joe is showing a student group how to read the emissions on a small screen, attached to a number of poles that stand across a small area of surface water and tufted grass. Apparently methane and carbon dioxide emissions are correlated and rise significantly over the water saturated areas. Thus, the nature of the land surface will determine the extent of emission. Joe explains that the active permafrost is approximately twenty centimetres deep at this point and that the permafrost itself continues down to one thousand feet before reaching the effects of earth's warm interior. Generally methane has a far higher emission near to the lakes, whereas the tufts of vegetation and the frost heave mounds produce a lower rate.

As with many scientists of climate change and its effects, Joe is still reluctant to jump to conclusions, but the emerging picture has an all too familiar message. Mapping the emissions and comparing results over a sequence of seasons will demonstrate an alarming increase in this potent greenhouse gas. Working on the tundra, beneath a blue sky and in seasonally high temperatures, one would be forgiven for imagining that the rising gas could be heard in the clear air.

The beauty of this work in the field is the immediacy of the recorded data as it flickers onto the screen, shaded from the direct sunlight. Methane and carbon

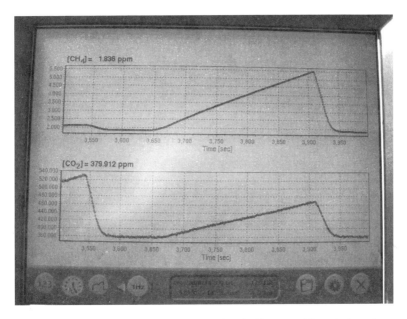

dioxide emissions rise on their respective graphical tables, resembling the heart beat monitor of a sick patient. As I stand looking at the screen I am aware of the breathing rate of the earth. Moving the pole sensors produces an intake of methane and carbon dioxide, and by hovering over the water and grass surfaces that breathing rate alters. A great lung, inhaling and exhaling, driven by a heart beat from earth's inner core.

19.7.2007. 8.45 hours.
Days at the Barrow Arctic Science Consortium are coming to a close and I decide on a revisit to the remote archaeological site at Point Barrow. The slender shingle spit stretching beneath the vast skies of the Arctic possess that essential simplicity that mirrors my thoughts on this northern land. Sometimes we have to eliminate much to get to that sense of place that lies beyond words. Here, the land runs out, roads end and the graves of early inupiat spill from that land into the anger of a rising sea.

Amid the confusion and noise of departure as the quad machines churn the shingle, I glance to seaward and there in the west a thin strip of sea ice cuts the horizon of ocean and sky. As we speed to the point, Santuro, one of the bear guides for the day, picks up and dispatches two king eider ducks that had become grounded upon the shoreline. Possibly they had become damaged during their long migration towards Canada.

Nearer to the point belugga whales can be seen close to the shore, as their white backs strain within the turbulent waters. The meeting of the two seas is marked by a clear line of division. Along the eastern shore the Beaufort Sea churns over a green density of water, whereas to the west the dark blue waters of the Chuckte Sea are interspersed by the white crests of breaking waves. Further out beyond this conversion zone of waters, the Arctic Ocean extends northwards like a shimmering plate within the uncertain movements of sea ice.

Perry is in a state of high excitement. Two eider kills and the prospect of the beluggas have energised him and he scampers around on his quad, taking in the various views to the east with Plover Point and to the west and the Chuckte Sea.

10.30 hours. His enthusiasm has ebbed sufficiently for him to be static and he reclines across his quad machine like a purring cat.

12.00 hours. A sketch of the field huts, as I sit upon the soft carpet tundra. Winds are increasing and the chill slows my progress and I decide to stop.

Perry and I head for Plover Point and the end of the spit. Seagulls and eider duck follow our progress along the shore and Perry concentrates his gaze on the beach for any vulnerable resting ducks. At the point belugga resurface, coming close to the shore. We recline on the quad and Perry recalls the whaling during the winter months of darkness. He tells of the early rise at four and the passage of the boats as they cut through the dark waters to the point.

Here at first light they set out for the bowhead and that first sight of a 'blow'. And then the chase with all boats in pursuit, heading out into the Arctic world of ice, until that first harpoon is thrown and the whale's fate is decided.

The dispatching of 'bombs', some at over a foot in length, may decide the death, but unless they strike the heart the kill is not immediate and it may take an hour before the great creature expires. Once dead, the whale is strapped, with a thick yellow band around the tail. Boats stay against the flanks to ensure that the whale will not slip out and sink. If this happens the whale will eventually inflate and rise to the surface, filling the air with its putrid decay. In this event blubber may be salvaged, but most of the body will be left for the orcas.

We stop at Plover Point for some time and I wander along the shore while Perry keeps his eyes trained across the turbulent water of the Beaufort Sea as the wind continues to rise. Standing on this northern shore I momentarily take compass points to east, west and south. To the south the entire land mass of America extends through its one hundred and thirty degrees of latitude before confronting the Straits of Magellan. At this point, upon a shifting spit where two seas sort and carry the shingle, I consider the prospect of its uncertain future.

15.00 hours. Returning to the site of the dig I take a walk by the still waters of the lagoon and come to a bone-strewn pool of caribou remains. A number of skulls lie within the clear water. It is a scene of slaughter, where the caribou may have been intercepted in their trail, only to die here on this lonely promontory.

15.30 hours. Back at the archaeological site a human skull has been uncovered from beneath the framework of whalebone. It appears to be a young adult, possibly female. The sight of the remains, beneath a sky of deteriorating weather, produces a silence across the area of the dig. For over eight hundred years these burial grounds have been left in peace and this cruel exposure beneath these leaden skies, upon a remote northern shore, has a great sadness.

I turn from the open graves as the group begin to load equipment and pack the bone specimens into boxes for the return journey. The wind has continued to increase and any belugga are now hidden within a white sea.

20.7.2007. 12.00 hours.
Departing from the science base I take the short ride with Scott along the coast to the settlement of Barrow and check in to the Top of the World hotel. Tour buses outside the hotel proudly proclaim top of the world tundra tours, and on this occasion they are not far from the truth. Within the narrow streets of Barrow there is the northernmost food store as well as the most northern police station on the American continent.

18.00 hours. I decide on Pepe's Restaurant, housed in what looks like a closed shed, and mistakenly go in the wrong door, to be ushered into an adjacent room, which looks very similar. Slightly confused, I sit down and order a pasta dish. As I await my meal an elderly lady with a large bow in her blonde hair places a dish of jelly and cream on my table, saying, 'free sweet for men on Friday'.

Out of the window I can see the streets of Barrow in early evening. Beyond the new police station occasional traffic disturbs the dust of the gravel roads. Along the streets and over the low roofs of the wood-built houses a forest of telephone poles and thick cables stretch across the backdrop of tundra expanse. The larger buildings that break this skyline are the new civic buildings of a community that is in transition.

I recall Perry's dismissive comments about the 'new' police, as earlier in the week a female polar bear and cub reached the Barrow shoreline from the distant sea ice, only to be fired upon and forced back out to sea. Apparently the elders would have let her rest before guiding her away from the community.

22.00 hours. I flick on the television in my room. Channels seem to merge into an endless kaleidoscope of soapy scenes and adverts, game shows and commercials. The big four by four vehicles are dominant in these commercials, featuring the Toyota Tundra and the Tundra Crewmax. These are the big part players in the changing perceptions of the land surface. That open page seen from the trampoline has been extended across a considerable portion of the northern tundra. The mystery and beliefs of the inupiat people are being rapidly translated into bland mileage.

21.7.2007. 9.00 hours. I take breakfast at the Osaki Sushi restaurant, across the street from the hotel. Sitting by the window, the grey tint of the glass presents a monotone view of the wood slatted sheds, interspersed by the large outlines of the four by four tundra landrovers. As I finish my coffee the top of the world tour bus rumbles across my view, followed by a tail of dust, as it dispatches a handful of tourists to the vastness of the tundra.

This afternoon I shall visit the recently constructed Inupiat Heritage Centre across the other side of town, but for now I take a walk around downtown Barrow. Much of the settlement consists of a ramshackle spread of wood-built structures, all in various states of deterioration.

I head down a grid of streets including Naavik, Nachik, Narook and Cake Eater (?). Doors are frequently left wide open in the summer season and the land is covered with snowmobiles, old engines and upturned sealskin boats, all littering the front gardens. Caribou and seal carcasses hang out to dry from the veranda and porch timbers. These untidy homesteads are all guarded by dogs and every plot has a chain snaking across the land among the debris. At the end of these rusty chains awaits a gilt-edged, hundred per cent certainty of canine-related death. Part of the growing up process in Barrow must, crucially, be the accurate calculation of chain length. Any miscalculation quite simply means no growing up process. I would like to think that there is a standard length of chain but something in my dark thoughts doubts this. The dogs of Barrow are the last line of defence against all invading forces, whether a particularly desperate thief or a polar bear.

Invasion on a more prolonged scale has afflicted Barrow in two waves. Initially, the Christian faith of the nineteenth century brought some solace to the long-held 'fatalism' of the inupiat, through education and medical care along with a day of rest to break the relentless season of the hunt. The more recent invasion from the oil dollar has been a more terminal affair, with its undermining of the inupiat way of life. In many ways this has been self-inflicted, cushioned by the gains of wealth and accompanied by the growing realisation of a change in climate.

14.00 hours. To the sound of barking dogs I approach the Inupiat Heritage Centre. This modern building housing a fine collection of objects and records of the people of the north coast stands separate from the homesteads at the edge of town.

I make for the whalers' gallery and soon become engrossed with the display. The accounts of whaling practices outline a sensibility that has been established between the whale and the inupiat. From the information cards attached to the old photographs I find that the elders relied upon an intimate knowledge of the seasonal changes in the ice. The combined flow of the two seas is unpredictable and the pack ice can go out or in, colliding with the land fast ice to cause an ivu or ice pile-up. Such collisions create major obstacles for the hunters, so that movements on the ice can become severely restricted. The vocabulary of the ice is intricate and includes such terms as sarri for big heavy ice, tuvuq for ice of the foreshore and sikuliaq for young ice.

The fading photographs show the whalers in their white clothing, made from the skin of wolf and lamb. With such camouflage, the hunters will not alarm the whale as it surfaces into the cold, white world of the ice and eventually enters the polynas of the ice, where the hunters would emerge from their tents for the kill. The whole process of the hunt exudes solemnity and a state of calm. The hunters have to be clean, as the whale is sensitive to human odours, and silent throughout the long wait and the death. Deep within the inupiat culture is the belief that the spirit of the whale will return and that the success of future hunting depends upon a respectful treatment of the hunted.

Moving slowly around the gallery I come to the area devoted to the polar bear and within a small glass case is a death pill. This object, the size of a golf ball, is made from coiled baleen with sharpened ends, and is placed in a chunk of blubber to be used as bait. The pill would spring open in the animal's stomach and puncture the intestines. Before the widespread use of the gun this was in common practice, but despite its obvious cruelty the display cards tell of the regard for the bear. When slain and skinned, the bear's windpipe was cut to release the animal's spirit. Inevitably, the centre has displays on the changing climatic conditions and glancing at the charts and figures of the seasons it is clear that the world of the inupiat is indeed fading away. Stormier weather, the loss of sea ice, eroding shorelines and a changing pattern of whale and caribou movements are all dismantling the lives of these people.

17.00 hours. I emerge from the centre into the bright sunlight of late afternoon and paddle along the shore of the Chuckte Sea. The water is cold, but only the numerous jellyfish deter me from attempting a swim. As I look out to an ice-free sea under a blue sky, it is difficult to assert where I am. At seventy-two degrees north, on the very tip of the American continent, barely eighteen degrees from the geographic North Pole, my feeling of disorientation is unsettling. It could be anywhere. The astonishing weather pattern of the past weeks could become 'norm' for the inupiat people. Their planar world of land and sea will fade as seas become less predictable and the methane-rich tundra proves to be unsuited for the caribou migrations.

I look along the eastern shore towards Point Barrow and the archaeological site. There, in the distant haze the early graves lie open as the sea claws back shingle. The wheel turns.

22.30 hours. I sit by the window and watch the extraordinary sight of two large grey whales close to the shore as they rub their broad sides upon the gravel beach. Beyond their rolling bodies I glimpse a long view into a future that is oceanic, spreading across the active waters like some new order.

22.7.2007. 9.00 hours.
Such are the gentle tides of the Chuckte Sea that the gravel beach displays the great indentations of the whale movements.

There is, however, a melancholy within these shingle beaches; the soft sounds of movement carried by these gentle seas as a summer season now unfolds. Within the streets of Barrow and along these low shores there are symbols and remnants of the fading culture. As I walk along the shore I come to a whalebone arch and look through the bleached, white structure to the north.

There is an irony in the fact that the inuits' understanding for the geography of the north is different from ours. They have little desire or reason to go further into

a cold world and would gladly remain in a land where food and survival were more secure. To the European explorers the extremity of the north had to be reached. These bones, however, are not about a compass point. They lead to a world of spirits, rather than a land surface. The door of the north elevates the soul, carrying it from this life to the next. The realm of the great aurora and the infinity of the polar skies are the dominion of the inuit north, high above the meaningless wastes of ice and time. The north is somewhere that you go after death, rather than in the fullness of life, and the south is a land that will only take you away from your ancestors. This shore is the end of the land. The whalers go perilously close to that other world when they venture onto the ice and this arch is a testimony to their faith.

My time in Barrow is coming to an end and I arrange a meeting with Dorcas Stein, curator and keeper at the Inupiat Heritage Center, to discuss the elements of the inupiat culture that have formed the basis of this faith.

From Dorcas's office within the heritage centre I can see across the rooftops of the sprawling communities of Barrow and Browerville to the blue surface of the Arctic Ocean.

Dorcas is an authority on inupiat culture and we run through the main pillars of belief. Apparently the role and significance of the shaman has declined from the high position of prophecy, although storytelling is still important in its animated form, much as Perry had performed in his conversations along at Point Barrow.

The inupiat concept of the land is based upon a nomadic practice that is applied to the vastness of the tundra. In this it is viewed solely as a means of survival. It is the way of the caribou. The sea is viewed as a garden where the coastal waters are plentiful in whale, seal and walrus, but entirely dependent upon the ice. The vast knowledge of ice passed down from the elders is the foundation of their culture and the recent uncertainty of sea ice, coupled with the variable migration of caribou, has serious implications on their ability to continue as a self-sufficient community.

My conversation with Dorcas, rather like that with Perry, crossed over from the bland realities of existence in this harsh environment to that other world. It had become a three dimensional dialogue. Dorcas, learned and impartial, continued to wander from one world to the other, but there was little doubt as to which world was fading. The inupiat and their old ways were fast moving into the past tense. As the conversation wavered, Dorcas outlined the strong belief in an animal intelligence. The animistic element was still strong and is encouraged in the schools through the drawing of the whale and the bear. I recall one group of children drawing depictions of the whale in mythology, where one of the drawings had been inscribed with the words 'the whales are listening'.

Nanuk, the bear, has always been a strong figure in the inuit culture and is rarely eaten. If the bear is killed, then those responsible would sew the eyes closed to prevent the bear from seeing the identity of the hunters.

My impression from the conversation is that the inupiat want to remain in that other world, but the bridge to it is melting before them, taking with it their link with land and animals.

Finally we address the question of climate change and it is apparent that the inupiat people see it as man's folly. The early communities of the north had developed an oral history of 'flood'. They have always known of the destructive world of water, remote as it is from the hard held realm of ice. For them the sea ice has become too thin and the extension of the land can no longer be relied upon. That extension had taken them to the animal spirits and their ancestors, and without the ice they and nanuk are both endangered.

15.00 hours. Housed next to the Inupiat Heritage Center is the Tizzy Consortium Library. I leaf through various books on inupiat drawings that depict their place within this strange landscape. I focus upon one particular drawing. It shows the latter stages of a whale hunt. The great bulk of the bowhead is fixed to the shore ice. The tail has already been removed and the cutting up of sections or shares can be

seen near the top of the page. Dogs leap at the approaching team of sledges and a bearded seal slides away from the scene of the hunt in a bid to escape. The drawing looks down on the hunt as if from a plane, yet also contains views from the level surface of the ice.

20.00 hours. Within the final moments on this shoreline I stand looking to the north. Repeatedly my gaze is drawn to the hard line of ocean, not to focus but to ponder the uncertainty that shrouds this shingle beach. During the past days I have stood here and noticed an elderly man taking a similar stance and looking out to sea. It may be that he is a whaler or a dignitary of the community. In his vigilance he is part of a long line of generations who have looked north from these lowly shores. However, unlike those earlier generations who saw the turning of the year dictated by the transformation of sea to ice, this solitary figure knows not the forthcoming sequence of events.

Part Five
The Orcadian Sea

The Orkney Islands

Sketch the Ninth.

'Still calm; made very little way; however the Fair-isle began to appear, Sanday and North Ronaldsay looking like threads along the surface of the water, tho' we sailed within a few miles of them.'

Tour through Islands of Orkney and Shetland. 1774. George Low.

Sketch the Tenth.

'On Ben Nevis a Mr Ormond was recording the event in the observatory near the top of the Ben. The violence of the gale caused constant pulsation of the air inside the room. All his instruments were being taken to the limit of their scale. When he went outside to get temperature readings from the screen he tied a rope around his waist but could not make headway. Later, he did reach the screen but could not read the figures due to the blinding drift lashing his face.'

The Great Storm. January 26. 1884. *Barry's History of Scotland.*

The Orcadian Sea.

The Orkney Islands. 2008.
Elevation. 50'
Latitude. 59 degrees north.

Journey to Kirkwall. 17.6.2008.
A weightless sea of mist fills the Moray Firth and the open waters of the North Sea. From the afternoon departure of the granite city of Aberdeen we head out beyond the tenuous stretch of the sea arm and into the grey swell of a northern ocean, heading north along the low profile of coast and eventually striking out to sea within the light of mid summer and the glide of gannets. Through the thinning mist, Rattray Head and the reaches of the firth shadow into a western horizon. About us the relentless grey waters, broken occasionally by the laced foam of a fallen wave. 18.30 hours. To the west the shapes of mainland and island are held within an anonymous geography of distance. In that uncertain gaze lie Stroma, the low contours of South Ronaldsay and the cluster of small islands that form the Pentland Skerries.

21.00hours. A first sighting of the island of Copinsay, close by and caught suddenly through the window of the ship's lounge. A large wedge of dark rock forming the eastern shore of the island and stretching along its kilometre length from Hinger Stone to North Nevi. As the ship passes the small island, so its form is revealed. From the north I look back and see the low rock and sand cord holding it to Cornholm and the diminutive Black Holm within the skerries. Like a dark sea swell the islands rise from the ocean surface as we pass, first Mull Head and then Rerwick Head, to negotiate the narrow channel of the 'String' and entry into the Bay of Kirkwall. In the fading light the islands can be seen stretching away to the north and west, low and subdued and resting within the dark waters.

18.6.2008. 16.00 hours.
With a steady fall of rain I find a solitary dry place beneath an overhang of rock. I have walked south from Kirkwall to Scapa Bay. The bay consists of a broad strand of sand that gives way to a rock shore.

From where I sit I look across the bay to the opposite shore. The land dips gently to these shorelines. Rain sounds upon the seaweed and the plastic flotsam that is scattered across the sand before me. Occasionally the cry of fulmar comes from the nesting areas that have been established above the rock overhang.

The islands are predominantly low-lying, and with the exception of their western margins where the power of the great Atlantic waters is met by the high terrain of Hoy, they are not dominated by the force of wave erosion. These are not dramatic shores. Inlets, bays and geos all dissipate the energy of the sea, so that any ingress from the rising waters is a gradual process of inundation. During the past 10,000 years the slow increase of temperatures has produced a sea level rise sufficient to flood the deep valleys and hills that had existed previously. The flood continues so that only the hill tops remain in the form of gentle slopes and rises that spread before me as I shelter from the rain. These islands exist within a rising ocean. They are held in a slow process of submergence that has brought them full circle through a world of lakes, ice and advancement from the sea.

19.6.2008. 8.00 hours.
I wake to the drumming of rain upon the skylight window. Within the small lounge conversation follows an inevitable course through weather and flood. The sound of bagpipes rises inexplicably from the street below.

During the winter persistent rain had produced flood in the streets of Kirkwall. Two days of torrential rain caused the local burn to be in spate. With the foul pool of Kirkwall full, further pressure came from a rising storm tide, so that the gate of the pool could not be opened. Subsequently the central part of the town was soon awash with a foul effluent sea of waste. Local reaction had been aimed at the gateman of the pool, though the insurance companies characteristically described it all as an act of God. Either way, it was a sequence of events that demonstrated the delicate balance that has been created by the meeting of human incompetence and the growing force of climate change.

10.00 hours. A quick visit to the internet café, where the computer screen displays various satellite maps of the weather situation for Scotland. As I click onto forecast, so the maps become animated with cloud movement. The entire area of Scotland is shrouded in a swirling white scarf of convecting air with few breaks. The archipelagos of Orkney and Shetland remain obscured upon the white screen.

13.00 hours. Defying the steady rainfall I catch a bus to the southern area of

Deerness. The road is straight, taking advantage of the flat land as it passes through a treeless landscape. Causeways link the small islands, and like a long necklace, the road eventually brings us to the island of Burray.

Walking from Echnaloch Bay I traverse the broad hillside that leads me to the small, uninhabited island of Hunda. Barely a mile in length and reaching its greatest height of forty metres, Hunda is typical of many of the islands. The gentle contours of the island are the crest of a hill, held within that slow drowning process. The long flood since the Pleistocene continues, and in all probability is now accelerating.

A hundred years ago Hunda had a population of seven. With poor grass it was unable to sustain more and as early as 1774 George Low had summed up the land as being of 'bad grass, much overrun with moss or "fog", which prevents the growth of good pasture.' By the 1930s it had become an uninhabited and barren holm, populated only by great terns, storm petrel and migrating eider duck. The shallow reef that joins it to Burray becomes submerged at high water and the island shrinks in its lonely isolation. Composed largely of boulder clay that rests upon the old elay flags of sandstone, the smooth-backed Hunda is predominantly a product of the departed glaciers.

Now, as I look down onto the broad back of the island, a steady rain obscures many of the shoreline rocks of sandstone. Hunda lies within a serene world of water, verdant with the fall of rain and unblemished by man. As the rain intensifies so the island recedes into the steel grey of distance. In between pulses of heavy rain I manage to sketch the outline of the island. Eventually I am forced to document the visit with photographs taken from various points. Tantalisingly the island fades and re-emerges with the passing rain.

I track back to Burray and visit the fossil and archive collection. Within the small museum the story of Hunda and the surrounding islands stretches back into a complex geological past. From the waters around Hunda prehistoric fish had been retrieved that indicated the earlier existence of a large freshwater lake. Long before the glaciers the island had been held within the warm tropical waters of Lake Orcadie.

As I depart from the museum the sky begins to lighten. The fields regain their fresh green tone from the grey monotone of the morning. Beyond the brow of the hillside Hunda lies serene and hidden in its silent anchorage within the deep waters of Scapa.

21.6.2008.
With an insufficient land mass to affect the pattern of weather, the islands are held within the hand of the ocean's atmospheric energy. Wind blows freely over the unhindered surface as the sea air devours the land.

11.00 hours. I stand at Skaill Bay on the western facing coast of the mainland of Orkney. It is a wide open bay facing due west across the broad back of the North Atlantic Ocean. The beach is strewn with torn kelp, its great journey east now halted upon this lowly shore. Grey sand displays the wave motions and indentations of the previous tide and the wind comes in powerful gusts from the breaking waves of an incoming tide.

The upper shore consists of slabs of the old flagstones, their gradual breakdown producing small discs that retain a warmth when held in the hand. As I head south a slight swell breaks over the lower ledges, like water pouring over stacked plates.

On the ruinous surface of the cliff tops, scree covered and cut into by steep sided geos, I pick up small bones of turnstone, fulmar and oyster catcher.

12.30 hours. I sit and spread the collection of bones on a slab of sandstone. Among the numerous match-like bones are the jaws of a shrew or field mouse, all probably the victims of the skuas that fly close to where I sit.

From Yasenby Stack I head north and return towards Skaill Bay. Taking a more landward path I come to the killing grounds of the skuas. Bones are arranged where the prey was dismembered. Eventually this light debris will be carried by flood

streams towards the cliff edge, as the waters cut into the sandstones. The relentless impact of the Atlantic swell and wave erosion have systematically worn back the flagstones during the period of rising sea level. Occasionally the imploding sound of a breaking wave rises from the base of the cliffs, detonating its force into the cracks and fissures of old rock.

22.6.2008. 8.00 hours.
I make my way through the rain-soaked streets of Kirkwall to the harbour to meet the morning departure for North Ronaldsay. The wind is coming from the south as a low pressure system moves rapidly north from the Pentland Firth. North Ronaldsay is the most northerly of the Orkney Islands, lying remote from the other islands at a latitude of 59 degrees north. As I approach the harbour I can see two passenger ferries preparing for departure to the Isles of Shapinsay and Eday. As I make my way through the lines of vehicles awaiting access to the car decks I am met by two port officials who inform me that the North Ronaldsay ferry has been cancelled due to the deteriorating weather conditions.

Storms increasingly dictate the movements between the islands and it is not unusual for the North Ronaldsay service, with its longer journey time and exposed course, to be cancelled, even in the summer months. The problem is not so much that of wave conditions as the swell within these northern waters. A large sea swell makes entry to the small harbour of North Ronaldsay particularly hazardous, if not impossible.

With the next ferry not due for three days I decide on the short flight and make my way to Kirkwall airport for the afternoon departure. Presented with the opportunity of a regular mail service and a steady stream of visitors, the residents of North Ronaldsay had seized the moment for an air link to Kirkwall in the early years of the twentieth century. In one day they had removed a thousand year old wall and cleared the fields of stones to enable the first flight to connect North Ronaldsay with the larger islands of the south.

14.00 hours. The small islander plane rises abruptly from Kirkwall. Below the islands spread out like lily pads afloat within a turbulent sea. Through the rain and low cloud I can make out their wave-breaking shores as light sands glow from beneath the water. With a quick stop at the island of Sanday, the plane reaches the windswept runway of North Ronaldsay. Across the gravel surface a small building serves as the airport terminal. Bags are unloaded and placed in the open doorway. As I pick up my rucksack the plane revs its engine noisily and races along the short runway for the return journey.

17.00 hours. I make my way towards the sands of Nouster Bay at the southern end of the island and cut through a break in the wall that serves as the sheep dyke. The island has over ten miles of coastline and this two-metre high wall extends around the entire island. The island's sheep are kept on the beach where they feed upon the kelp. As I glance across the open fields I can see walls extending across the width of the island. For over a thousand years these walls and the sheep dyke have defined the island into a matrix of small holdings and common land.

However, the storms of January 1993 caused considerable damage. Three kilometres of the dyke were washed away in a rising tide. The Iron Age settlement of Burian Broch on the southern tip of land sustained damage to its four-metre thick walls and is now at risk from the combined effect of rising sea level and a growing intensity of storms. The same storm caused havoc on the nearby island of Sanday, where the rising waters almost cut the island into two sections.

During the stormy January of 1993, 21 days recorded gale force winds as roads on Hoy were washed away and the Scrabster to Stromness ferry took 8 hours to complete what is normally a 2-hour journey. Kirkwall spent much of the month under a foot of water and as the winds rose 21 January recorded 129 mph at Flotta before going off the scale.

As I clamber down to the beach I can see Burian Broch at the far reach of the bay. In bright sunlight I walk along the sands of the broad bay towards a group of grey seals. Fulmar shelter along the base of the dyke wall, and the diminutive sheep scurry over the flat surface of the rock ledges.

23.6.2008. 7.00 hours. I wake to the sound of wind, as clouds race across the small skylight. From the windows of the hostel I can see the hard horizon of blue-grey ocean, speckled with the white of breakers. The low contours of the island create the sensation of being within an open boat. Sea and sky are close, with little to divide them.

As I make my way along the straight road that acts as a backbone to the island that feeling of being at sea remains with me. My walk continues in a north-easterly direction as the sun rises into an almost cloudless sky. From Ancum Loch the land mass extends eastward to the lighthouses. At the old beacon, now shrouded in scaffolding, the land gives way to an expansive shore of flagstones, ledges and the low profile of Seal Skerry lying beyond the island coastline. Circling Dennis Head, I step from ledge to ledge to the furthest point and look back at the old beacon, standing within five metres of the high water mark. After its construction in 1789 it served for only twenty years before being decommissioned. Its stature was insufficient for the shipping routes that used these northern seas.

An incoming tide is washing over the flagstones, as the offshore breakers indicate the lower ledges and an old shoreline. As I return to the upper shore I step up over successive ledges, each signifying a notch within the long tide of sea level rise. Walking towards the new beacon, pulses of rain blow across from the south-west. The insular nature of the showers can be seen as the trails of the systems are dragged over the low profile of the land.

14.00 hours. Leaving the northern coast of the island I continue along the western boundary, keeping to seaward of the sheep dyke. Torness Plateau rises gradually from the almost uniform surface of North Ronaldsay. It is the highest point of the

island, with burial grounds and standing stones at its apex. This rise of land may one day be the last remnant of the island with its windswept surface of poor grass and scattered stones.

15.00 hours. As the afternoon passes and I continue on my circular walk around the island, so I begin to realise how narrow is the area in which the shore and ledges exist. The fate of the island rests within a band of rock barely reaching fifteen feet in height. North Ronaldsay is contained precariously within this perimeter of crumbling rock. It is at the limit of its defence from a rising sea.

23.00 hours. I look out from the bird observatory. Like an ocean swell, the islands of Papa Westray and Westray lie low on the horizon. Only the beacon, sending its light into the late evening sky, breaks the horizontal line of sea and sky. These are vulnerable islands, seemingly afloat in the uncertain hold of the sea.

24.6.2008. 8.00 hours. Perfect stillness in the early morning. Towards Westray silent breakers beneath a street of high cumulus cloud. Before my departure from the island I walk along Nouster Bay. Sheep scamper over the upper shore, producing a deep chime upon the rocks. I sit for a while at Burian Broch.

Looking towards Brideshess Point, I can see the wall of the sheep dyke extending in a broad arc around Brides Ithy. At some time, in a future of rising waters, this old wall will form the first line of resistance to the mounting intensity of the North Atlantic storms.

12.00 hours. Depart North Ronaldsay. Flight to Kirkwall and Stromness.

25.6.2008. 19.00 hours.
From the bar of the Stromness Hotel I look out across Clestrain Sound with its cluster of skerries, narrowing into the turbulent waters of Bring Deeps. Visibility has been poor throughout the day ,but with the rise of the low cloud I can see the base level of the coast of Hoy across the sound.

As I study the map I read of places that are hidden within the wall of light rain. Bring Head, Candle of the Sale and White Breast trail along the Hoy coastline, while the island of Rysalittle lies close to the shore, with its own narrow waters of Rysa Sound. Bring Deeps fills with white crests as the wind increases through the Sound of Hoy.

26.6.2008. 9.00 hours.
Cloud level has risen sufficiently to see the heights of the island of Hoy. The margin of existence that I had noticed in North Ronaldsay, with its apparent make do approach to the problem of sea encroachment, is displayed along much of the island's coastline. As I walk along the shores of the Hoy sound I come to a patchwork of sandbags that have been placed within the fragmenting sandstone of the upper shore. Close by these sea defences an old stone wall encloses a cemetery. Many of the headstones are inscribed with readings of latitude and longitude, indicating that the buried were probably mariners. High and dry upon the shores of the sound, the seamen rest: the sea had taken them and in the fullness of time it will claim them back.

11.00 hours. The northern headland of Hoy displays a methodical and relentless breakdown by the force of the sea and I decide on a number of sketch studies from various points along the coast. From each of the sketching locations it is clear that the sea has weakened and exposed the cracks and joints within the sandstones, producing an almost geometric breakdown. As I draw low cloud moves across the higher slopes of Hoy. Like a sheet being dragged off of an old chair, the low cap of cloud moves from the rugged head. Once the cloud has been lifted so the craggy details of the headland become exposed to the full light of day. However, my attempts at drawing the Hoy headland become a dialogue of various views and partial glimpses as the afternoon sun is interspersed by layers of cumulus cloud. Kame of Hoy, Slett of the Head and Muckle Head come and go within the procession of the weather.

Consequently the drawings become a summary of the main slopes and contours of the head, drifting between the imagined and the real.

15.00 hours. Returning through the streets of Stromness, a glance down one of the narrow streets draws my attention to the Orkney College of Marine Studies. It is a line of investigation that leads me eventually to Professor Jon Side of the International Centre for Island Technology (ICIT). A resident of Stromness for almost twenty years, Jon has been studying changes to the environment through research into marine and terrestrial systems. One of the more alarming features has been the collapse or 'crash' of a number of bird groups, specifically the auks and arctic terns. As a result of these crashes they have now ceased to fledge within the islands and subsequently stay for far shorter periods of time.

One reason for this changing pattern has been the drop in sand eels, due to over-fishing and more specifically the altered strength of the North Atlantic Conveyor. The warm waters of the conveyor have a direct effect upon the frequency of storms and the intensity with which these events are inflicted upon the northern islands. They also bring a different content of water, with variations in plankton. A fall in plankton may be the main cause for the fall in the sand eel. Jon explains that parallel with the fall of the sand eel is the rise in diet of pipefish. Seabirds such as guillemots and auks line their nests with the dry remains of the pipefish. Any nutritional value from this fish is low.

The North Atlantic Conveyor now flows with a greater volume through the narrow channels of the islands, entering the open waters of the North Sea and reaching as far as the Baltic. Water temperatures and water content are now establishing new patterns of marine life as well as life in the air.

Professor Jon Side believes that the ocean currents are a root cause behind these various changes and that the trigger of environmental and climatic fluctuation may well lie in the depth of the oceans. For the present time isolated phenomena are finding their way into the reports of the Orcadian newspapers. Recently sea bass have been caught by the fleet and Mediterranean fish are now being unloaded regularly upon the harbour stones of Stromness.

30.6.2008. 11.00 hours.
Boat from Stromness to Hoy. Rackwick and the broad bay facing the open waters of the Northern Atlantic. As I stand on the upper shore the landscape of Hoy before me displays the departure of the glaciers. To the east I look into the wide gape of a valley carved by the movement of ice. In the foreground moraines are spread across the valley floor, while scree and steep slopes define the area of direct ice contact. The present valley holds the narrow course of South Burn, fed by the waters from the higher slopes.

Leaving the valley, I climb the northern flank towards Moor Fea and the Geo of the Light. From the heights I can see the extent of the terminal moraine spread within the valley below. Beyond the rolling terrain of clays and glacial boulders, the flat floored valley clearly indicates the scale of the glacier in its slow descent towards the Atlantic waters.

Earlier I had seen a group of walkers making for the southern cliff of Rackwick Bay. They had moved slowly up the steep cliff, but as I look now assisted with binoculars they are lost within the immensity of the headland. Large areas of Hoy are over a thousand feet in altitude, contrasting it with the other, low-lying islands of Orkney. Due to the nature of the hills of Hoy, with their convex slopes, my line of vision to the shore becomes broken and only occasionally am I able to see the sheer rock of the cliffs. Approaching the Geo of the Light, skuas glide past and the sound of the constricted waters rise from the narrow inlet. The west coast of Hoy is broken by numerous geos as the full force of Atlantic waves drills into the weakened sandstones.

13.00 hours. Beyond the stack of the Old Man of Hoy I continue to the higher cliffs and Ward Hill. From the heights of the island it is possible to envisage the size of the ice cap that would have covered these hills throughout the glacial period, adding its weight to the land during the long winter.

14.00 hours. As I reach the Sleet of Heel, so a bad moment unfolds. I wander off track and am forced to descend a steep heather slope to Leanders Dale, while skuas swoop to defend their nesting areas and it begins to rain.

18.30 hours. Eventually I depart Hoy as great columns of rain fill the central glacial col, sending the heights of Ward Hill into a low grey cloud. The whale-back hills of Hoy fade into the weightless infinity of convecting air.

1.7.2008. 11.45 hours.
Stromness to Scrabster. Through the Sound of Hoy, rounding the bulk of the northern headland, the precipitous walls of rock that I had sketched from the coast of the main island now stand darkened by the percolation of water through the old sandstones.

Following the west coast of Hoy and the high cliffs of Sleet of the Heel, Bre Brough, St John's Head, we pass the Old Man and continue to Rora Head. A geo-riven wall of rock trails south along ten miles of unrelenting collision with the forces of the sea. This is the line of resistance for the Orkney Islands. To the east beyond this towering island the low profiles of Flotta, South Ronaldsay and Burray languish in the subdued waters awaiting a slow and relentless inundation.

The Orcadian Sea and the islands of Orkney present us with a window onto an uncertain future. Within their low-lying interiors are lands barely higher than the breaking waves that define their shorelines. Storms increasingly threaten these fields of Orkney and future surges from higher seas will surely marginalise the islands beyond the balance of man's effective usage.

From the deck of a southbound ferry many of the islands are now hidden from view, lying below the curvature of the earth within the broad hold of the ocean. Many areas of mainland Britain, though far from the remote waters of this northern archipelago, face a similar future. Extensive stretches of Britain's eastern shoreline face the North Sea from the moderate heights of boulder clay, left like an afterthought by the great retreat of the Pleistocene ice. This open back door exposes hundreds of miles of coast to the uncontrollable volume of the North Sea.

My travels within the Orkney Islands have focused my concern on a simple equation: the combination of wave height and sea level and the contour characteristics of the individual islands. This key balance, by all accounts is in a process of alarming adjustment, if the predictions of the potential eustatic level are accurate. Within the recent accounts and timing of the island storm sequences lie the dynamics of storm events and their impact upon the individual communities. Freak storms such as that of 1884 tend to be absorbed into a folklore, allowing people to rebuild and continue with their lives. But when the frequency increases as well as intensity, it can break even the most resilient of spirits. In this sense I suspect that the great cultures of early history have 'gone' to the force of climatic pressure with its incessant impact. Human nature, even when confronted with earthquake and volcanic action, manages to hold on. The prospect of a slow rising tide and the breaking of shorelines is, however, an ever-present fear. In this respect the sea is vast, persistent and uncompromising.

At some future point the cartographer's art will be called upon to redraw the coast of Britain, and within that distant projection these islands will occupy the greater waters of a northern ocean.

2.7.2008. 10.00 hours. Before beginning my journey south I visit the North Highland College, based in Thurso, which includes the Environmental Research Institute. Various aspects of the implications of climate change are studied at the college and I am met by Priyanka Sharma, the business, development and commercialisation manager. It is clear that the area faces a number of challenges, including the utilisation of the Pentland Firth as an energy source. Priyanka leads me down the corridors of the old school building and through heavy doors to a room marked 'climate change'.

Much of the research at the college has been supported by the Tyndall Centre for Climate Change, and the work of John Coil and David Woolf has focused upon the sensitivity of the Western Isles of Scotland to changes in wave and wind climate. Within this study, satellite altimetry and gale frequency have been used to assess wave and wind responses to the North Atlantic Oscillation (NAO). The region studied is regularly exposed to the easterly tracking Atlantic storms, many of which originate from the Newfoundland sea area. A high index on the oscillation leads to a storm where wind speeds may exceed forty knots and wave heights increase significantly. The study has shown that the high latitudes of 60-90 degrees have experienced a poleward shift of extra-tropical cyclonic activity due to hemispheric warming. The warming process has a number of repercussions, and in my conversations with David Woolf he explains that with the loss of sea ice, sea conditions can also change. Effectively, no ice means a greater 'fetch' from the north and therefore the scale of sea swell will rise.

The deep extra-tropical depressions are particularly intense, as was seen in the storms of January 2005. The exceptional storm of 11 and 12 January followed a period of deep depressions that had tracked east from Iceland. Two weeks prior to the storm, sea conditions had been very severe. The climax of the storm saw ferry disruption, road damage, pier and house damage and general chaos. This was an intense storm and the indications are that the strength of wind and wave activity will continue to increase. The report on the research programme had come to the conclusion that the sea state is indeed sensitive to the North Atlantic Oscillation. The implications for the ferry companies and the general economy of the north-west are serious.

Within the climate change laboratory I am introduced to Sarah Crowe, who has been studying Peatland Ecological Processes in the context of the climatic and environmental implications. At the outset it is clear that the climate change taking place today is far more rapid than the warm interglacial periods of earlier times. As we are the only change within those periods of time, we are probably the cause of the greater carbon emissions of today. Recent news that the far north may be free of ice this season adds weight to the argument.

From our conversation it is clear that the Peatlands play an important part in climate change, particularly within these higher latitudes of the Northern

Hemisphere. Their conservation is a priority issue, and as I leave the college I am given some of the research publications on the Peatlands of Caithness and Sutherland.

3.7.2008. 7.00 hours. The train departs from Thurso on its journey to Inverness. It is a journey that will take me across the peatlands. As I begin to gloss over the strategy programme for 2005-15 we begin to encounter the rolling terrain of gorse and heather.

The 'flow country' spreads out like an ocean. A number of bog ponds and lochs are interspersed between wide surface areas of grey and green. 10.00 hours. The train passes through Helmsdale and follows the coast to Brora. A sea coloured with the peat rich waters washes its umber breakers over the shore.

The destruction of the peat and the emission of carbon can occur from a number of circumstances. The earlier forestation of the area had led to higher emissions due to burning and tree failure within the soft ground. Attempts at draining had also proven to be damaging on the fragile ecosystem. Drains would accelerate erosion and downcutting, which in turn led to a drying out of the surface.

The emphasis of conservation of the 'flow country' is clearly to protect and maintain its water content. As I look from the train window I consider the similarity of the terrain to that of the present-day tundra of the far north. Ten thousand years ago, when the ice left this area, it is probable that it left a frozen, periglacial surface. By the same process, today's tundra is being transformed to the bogland of some future warmer world.

The warming belt of climate change moves ever northward, like the path of sunlight replacing shadow. That glacial sequence of freeze and thaw has moved across the surface many times in the past. As it nears the polar regions, so the significance of the exposed peatlands, with their rich store of carbon, becomes more apparent.

Two weeks of travelling within the Orcadian archipelago and one may be forgiven for not registering the big changes of the global climatic model. The spectacular ice melt of the far north and the frenzied activity of the hurricane belt within the lower latitudes are far from these islands.

But there is something intrinsically different in the air and sea. For the patient observer the pulse of change can be touched, for the signs are there. It is within the visible manifestations of the natural world. The simple observation of the movement of birds and the sight of a rare fish pulled from the net of a North Atlantic trawler.